SOCIAL
CASE RECORDING

SOCIAL
CASE RECORDING

BY

GORDON HAMILTON

SECOND EDITION

PUBLISHED FOR
THE NEW YORK SCHOOL OF SOCIAL WORK
BY COLUMBIA UNIVERSITY PRESS
NEW YORK : MCMXXXVIII

PREFACE

THIS book was undertaken because of the constant demand in the field of social case work for illustration and discussion of practices in recording. If we are to study case work we must perforce study whole records to follow the development of people in an observed experience; but if we wish to study various kinds of expressions and compositions in case work, we may, allowing for the limitations of fragments, make some use of short passages.

Acknowledgment is gratefully made to the following agencies which have permitted the use of their material: The Bobs Roberts Hospital, Chicago; The Children's Aid Society of New York City; The Connecticut Children's Aid Society; The Emergency Home Relief Bureau of New York City; The Emergency Relief Administration of New Jersey; The Family Welfare Association of America; The Family Society of Philadelphia; The Institute for Child Guidance of New York City; The Institute of Family Service of the Charity Organization Society; The Jewish Board of Guardians of New York City; The Jewish Social Service Association of New York City; The Michael Reese Hospital of Chicago; and The Presbyterian Hospital of New York City.

Acknowledgment is also made to the wide circle of agencies which have so generously permitted their records to be examined. A peculiar difficulty attaching to this study is that many whole records which reveal admirable case work control do not lend themselves to excision of portions for illustration.

The writer is indebted to various members of the faculty of the New York School of Social Work and to Miss Christine C. Robb, formerly Chief of Social Service, The Institute for Child Guidance, New York City, for reading parts of this manuscript and to Miss Mabel P. Ashley for assistance in its preparation. I am especially indebted to Mr. Porter R. Lee, Director of the School, and to Miss Anna Kempshall, Director of the Institute of Family Service of the Charity Organization Society, for their technical criticism and helpful suggestions.

GORDON HAMILTON

New York
March 2, 1936

PREFACE TO SECOND EDITION

IN PREPARING a second edition of this book I have taken
the opportunity to correct the text in several places, to
add a few new illustrations, and especially to clarify the
terminology with regard to the main recording forms.
This book is neither a manual nor a scientific treatise.
It reflects the observations of a student of case work, but
is not a book on case work. I have been asked why I
have not given my point of view explicitly as to how to
write records. Although I have, by selection and emphasis, frequently expressed my preferences for this or
that method, my point of view remains simply this: that
records are written for use; that there is no one way to
write records; and that although good case workers are
not always good recorders, there are no good records
except those written by good case workers. There is, I
believe, room for a wide variety of record styles, no one
of which is likely to be more right than another, and
probably a combination of methods is the most desirable consummation.

In addition to new illustrations of periodic summaries, treatment evaluations, and group "process,"
Chapter IX, Recording in Public Assistance, has been
rewritten to conform more closely to conditions in
public-assistance agencies, and a Glossary of Recording
Terms has been appended. I have permitted myself
more illustrations of the "process" style than of other
styles, because it is still the most interesting experi-
ment; but I am sure that within the next few years we

shall see marked improvement by means of omissions, selection, and condensation, an eclectic approach to the recording of history and treatment, and in consequence we shall have records characterized by emphasis upon diagnosis and clearly defined services and therapy.

Acknowledgment is due for additional material to the Judson Health Center, the Neurological Institute, the Institute for Family Service, of the Charity Organization Society, and the Jewish Social Service Association, all of New York City; to the Department of Welfare, Old Age Assistance, Allegheny County, Pennsylvania; and also to the Family Welfare Association of America for permission to reprint an excerpt from *Differential Approach in Case Work Treatment*; to the University of Chicago Press for reprinting an excerpt from *Psychiatric Social Service in a Children's Hospital.*

GORDON HAMILTON

New York
March 1, 1938

CONTENTS

I

INTRODUCTION

THE best way, undoubtedly, to study recording is to read as many case records as possible. In addition to the case records available in different types of agencies, records have from time to time been published[1] either separately or in book form, and these may be used to aid in forming judgments as to method and structure, as well as to the nature of case work itself. The attempt to display recording methods through illustration and interpretation, though difficult, may be justified in particular for those who do not have ready access to a variety of records.

The purpose of keeping a case record has been adequately described by Sheffield[2] and others and needs no special elaboration here. The primary purpose of the record is to improve the quality of service to the client and to help us understand him and his situation. Social case workers, even more than most professional people, are peculiarly dependent on documents for their daily practice, and, since the nature of the social case cannot easily be demonstrated to students by direct observa-

[1] The earliest case records prepared in 1911 by Mary Richmond for the Russell Sage Foundation and privately printed are no longer available. In conjunction with the *Social Service Review*, The University of Chicago Press has published *Medical Social Case Records*, with introduction by S. P. Breckinridge, 1928. Samples of whole case records may be found in *Social Case Work*, by Cannon and Klein, published by the Columbia University Press, and in other publications. See Bibliography.

[2] Sheffield, Ada E., *Social Case History, Its Construction and Content*, Russell Sage Foundation, 1934.

tion and attendance, as in ward medicine, the workers must use documents to extend their range of knowledge. Moreover, the nature of the social case itself, fluid, formless (the matrix being nothing less than the totality of a life organization) is so complex that the situation and treatment must be carefully described, or many clumsy, painful, and unnecessary treatment gestures may occur. Not only is it impossible to carry a great quantity of case details in one's mind, but as social work is organized today within agencies rather than private practice, there is a group use of the record which makes lucid, concise, and accurate recording indispensable.

In spite of the need which most of us have of finding rules and procedures to guide us, we must face the difficulty at the outset that there is no such thing as a model record, no routines which will make the case inevitably clear, accessible, and understandable. Records should be written to suit the case, not the case geared to a theoretical pattern. There are no canons of mass or coherence, no dramatic unities to which the living human situation must be shaped. The case record may be used for a number of purposes (administrative, treatment, study, teaching, research), and each purpose will condition the arrangement of its component parts.

In the sort of case record kept in many colleges the student is individualized by descriptive material, ratings, grades, and so forth, but the treatment focus is absent. Likewise in certain psychological records, the photographs, examinations, and observations are made with little reference to treatment. In the social sciences the tendency is always to try to isolate measurable units which can be classified and for which predictions and generalizations may be made. Records may be found which rely heavily on laboratory findings, psychometric tests, and even attitude and aptitude tests. Data are reported objectively concerning both setting and behavior, and little or no attempt at interpretation is made. The facts largely speak for themselves. The social case record, however, is always centered on treatment purposes and the emphasis will be placed on selection, evaluation, and diagnostic thinking. The more treatment there is in a record, the more likely it will tend to diagnostic process throughout. Individual records today, however, vary greatly in the weighting given to factual data and to interpretation. "Comprehension" is perhaps a philosophic rather than a scientific exercise, but all the better case records show both the discipline of facts and the discipline of elicited meaning.

We shall not here attempt to describe the administrative purpose of records. In earlier days the case record was a sort of omnibus affair designed not only to show what was done for the client but to show effort, "production," business transactions, appointments, and other administrative concerns now properly kept elsewhere. The trend has been to relieve the case record of the necessity of bookkeeping, bill collecting, relief accounts, the number of visits or telephone calls made or letters written, and to transfer these and other kinds of case accounting to appropriate reports and indices. Readers interested in these secondary forms of recording may consult several useful texts.[3] We shall not de-

[3] Clark, Mary Augusta, *Recording and Reporting for Child Guidance Clinics,* The Commonwealth Fund, 1930. Fisk, Helen I., *Statistical Recording and Reporting in Family Welfare Agencies,* Family Welfare Association of America, 1934.

vote much attention, moreover, to the uses of the record for study, teaching, and research, although we shall give this subject brief consideration. Our preoccupation will be throughout with the ordinary practice or treatment record as found in any social case work agency.

Most workers would agree that the case record is not about individuals[4] in the biological sense but individuals as they find themselves or fail to find themselves in society. The stress on personal treatment or environmental manipulation; on self-direction or on social responsibility will vary with different workers and different cases. Variations in the content and emphases within social case work seem to be quite directly reflected in the recording style. That this is somewhat accidental and as much the result of imitation as of conscious selection of medium does not change the probability that there is an inherent affinity between content and form of expression. In the last analysis, however, the writer must decide what tools, what constructions, and what style best suit the case material and best reveal its significance. During the twenties the phrase "social case work" began to be used for the generic case work idea in recognition of total socio-psycho-biological life organization. Current practice, however, although roughly generic is constantly modified by a number of factors: traditional field distinctions still

[4] Sheffield, Ada E., *The Situation As The Unit of Social Case Study*, Social Forces, June, 1931. Here Mrs. Sheffield says the "situation" is the unit of work "in which the individual or the family figures within an aggregate of interactive and interdependent factors of personality and circumstance." And again, "Within the situation the social process as served by the worker is usually one of successful or unsuccessful maturing in the formative relations between the client, the circumstances, and other people involved." She proposes a direct concern with the objective experience of the client.

existent, partly because of inertia and lack of a common professional training; administrative restrictions of public or private agencies, or of community or institutional auspices; the infiltration of more psychiatric concepts in some areas than in others; cultural patterns in some places and technical rituals in others, all make it impossible to select records completely typical of anything. An attempt has been made in the chosen illustrations to give generic focus and structure for which administrative adaptation is always to be assumed. The points made, if true at all, should be true in any field.

This book then concerns itself mainly with a presentation from generic practice, with little space devoted to the adaptations of different fields. A physical and mechanical problem lies in the necessity for piecemeal illustration. To reproduce enough of the case record to show a long study or a continuous piece of treatment is impracticable. It is hard to answer the question, "Is it good recording?" without becoming involved in the question, "Is it good case work?" We shall give illustrations intending to answer the question, "Is this a valid way of attempting to show a situation, or a piece of executive handling, or an interacting relationship or an evaluation?" but we shall assume that it is not relevant to argue from small cross-sections arbitrarily selected, whether or not the case or the interview is well handled. Indeed if the written statement is clear enough to provoke discussion as to the invalidity or validity of the handling, it will serve at least one appropriate purpose of the record, namely, the supervisory or teaching purpose.

This book will then demonstrate the topics of general format and structure of case records, chronological entries and summaries, diagnostic and evaluational material, letters and reports, and differences in style. A special chapter is devoted to adaptations of recording in the field of public assistance, since this has been subject to such rapid expansion within the last six years as to excite many questions from workers. Also, attention is given to the problem of recording treatment process because of current developments in this difficult and experimental area. Ideally the record is designed to project our observations and check upon our observations; to include the classification and arrangement of material; our relationships to our material, that is, persons and their situations; the formulation of our hypotheses; the treatment process and experience; and the appraisal of results. One of the factors which makes records hard to read and to use is that of clumsy or inadequate physical organization, and we shall therefore make this the first point of our discussion.

II

FORMAT AND STRUCTURE OF THE RECORD

THE ordinary case record in most social agencies is typewritten on one or both sides of 8½x11 sheets and bound in a cheap but strong Manila folder. Twenty years ago records were much less convenient. Often hand written, or on half sheets of paper loosely clipped together, or worse still, folded and placed in an envelope, they were not designed for ready reference. The origin of the phrase "red tape" is sometimes ascribed to the Civil War veterans' records which were placed in envelopes and tied with yards of tape cumbersome to deal with. The modern record, firmly held together by one of several reliable devices, opens flat like a book. Occasionally records for particularly heavy use, such as hospital records, will have a thick cardboard binding, but for most purposes the Manila folder is sufficient. It is recognized that records are for use and that the time spent in reading a record may be more costly than the time spent in setting it up. For this reason convenience and readability in form as well as in content are requisite. Departmentalized agencies are accustomed to bind their several contributions separately and place all in an envelope folder from which each portion can be withdrawn, but this is less desirable than the unit record, so integrated that all the contributors to the record will have the opportunity and stimulus of reading the whole case.

The purpose of records conditions the structure and content. Case records may in varying degrees serve the purpose of the treatment of the client, administration, teaching, and research. Mrs. Sheffield[1] defines record purposes as treatment, social betterment, and assisting the case worker in critical thinking. In the main the focus of this text will be the record as a tool in treating the client, although other purposes will be recognized in a special chapter.

The record commonly contains a face sheet, history or narrative sheets, correspondence, and, in addition, such special forms as budget, health, business, home economics, or similar outlines, and also forms for child placement, relief cards, or records of board paid. Extreme variation in the arrangement and selection of outlines in agency practice, however, makes illustration impracticable. There is a general tendency to omit from the folder items that have largely an administrative significance, as for instance the cash or ledger card; not to file bills or business matters, but to handle such documents in separate files.[2] The "index of effort" and "overhead" items, telephone calls, number of appointments, need not be kept in the case record in "behold-me-busy" entries, but may be efficiently recorded on day sheets or other accounting devices. Records are then freed to serve their primary purpose.

The Face Sheet

The face sheet has the purpose of giving identifying data about the persons concerned in the social situa-

---

[1] Sheffield, A. E., *The Social Case History*, Russell Sage Foundation, 1934.

[2] In relief agencies financial data cards containing the budget and changes in the rate of relief may be left in the front of the folder or in an appropriate box on the worker's desk. Periodic entries as to the rate and amounts of relief supplied by the accounting departments should appear in the record, as well as the budget.

tion. Names, addresses, occupations, relatives, citizen-ship, nationality, religion, birth and marriage dates, social status (that is, whether single, married, or divorced) , are intended to distinguish this particular person and this family from others of the same name. A secondary purpose, also locating and identifying, is shown on face cards under such headings as "ward" or "clinic," "district," "precinct," "social worker," which tend to locate the patient administratively in the agency rather than in society at large. Some people state that the face card should outline "the social situation at a glance." This seems less accurate than to say that the face card gives in convenient form certain objective social facts of a more or less permanent character which particularize this case. Registering students for colleges, or citizens for voting, or applicants for employment or hospital care is a quite obvious process. In the course of a lifetime one is frequently registered. Since registration may be done by clerical assistants, it is wise not to feature intimate facts or highly ephemeral material on a face card. The card should be so arranged as to permit easily of change of address, or of school, or place of employment without making a fresh card at short intervals. Although a face card may be the basis of agency statistics, an index type of card is also employed in most agencies. The face sheet may be a simple edition of the index card and copied from that, or vice versa. The index cards may be used as a central file and social statistics may be conveniently posted from such cards.

In agencies which use an application blank, there may be duplication among the data on the blank, the face sheet, the financial data sheet and the index card. Care should be taken to have no more overlapping forms than are absolutely indispensable and to arrange identical material on blanks uniformly so as to facilitate copying.

Face sheets should at a minimum have enough data to clear through a social service exchange or central index. A maximum is harder to state, but nothing should be on a face sheet which is not likely to be referred to from time to time, and face sheets should be simple, accurate, and up-to-date. Administrative identifying data will vary with the function of the agency. In child placing work, especially, the last address of the child and responsible guardian must be currently registered. The names and addresses of more than one relative are convenient as a means of locating families which move frequently. It is no longer thought necessary to put medical diagnoses[3] or intelligence ratings on the face sheet. It is better for such material to go on a separate sheet with enough interpretation to make the classification useful. Social diagnoses are inherently too long to be placed on the face sheet and should be in the text. A few agencies dealing with transients add "marks" or "scars" to the ordinary social identification because of the prevalence of aliases, but such a practice borders on police work rather than normal case work procedure. Social Service Exchange clearings may be typed on the face sheet or on the history sheet. The slips should not be kept, but if kept, should be pasted in.

THE HISTORY SHEETS

The face sheet may be followed, as in the record form common in child guidance clinics, by separate "work-

---

[3] Disabilities are quite commonly found on face sheets when agencies are concerned with problems of employability, but one should be cautious of labeling conditions which may not be permanently or even significantly descriptive.

ups" of medical, psychiatric, psychological, and social studies, or may be followed by the social notes alone. The word "history" is still somewhat loosely used to cover either the whole case narrative or merely the initial stages of social study which include background and personal history of the client and his family (anamnesis). Whether the main text should be carried forward in topical or chronological style, we shall discuss later. Some records have sheets of various colors for special topics, and in the so-called "unit record" in hospital or child guidance work in which several professions make entries, the problem of departmentalized structure suggests the use of paper in various colors. In ordinary social case records too variegated a color scheme may be confusing. Most workers do, however, prefer some colored sheets in the text to indicate diagnostic discussion or other important features.

Correspondence

Letters which relate to the treatment of the client may be interleaved with the text or else filed consecutively at the end of the record. In either event the consensus of opinion is that the text should include an entry as to the nature of the letter, i.e., "Letter received from John Smith about Patrick's classroom problems," rather than merely, "Letter received." The entry should not be more than a line or two, since for details the reader should consult the correspondence itself. Probably it is slightly preferable to file letters (if a number are exchanged) at the end. In agencies whose main function is correspondence the letters themselves may constitute the text. Abstracts and reports exchanged between social agencies are usually interleaved at the time received.

Records are occasionally embellished by photographs, or, if psychometric tests are used, the original test material may be preserved as well as the interpretation. Care should be taken to distinguish significant from insignificant material in order not to clutter the text. Christmas and Easter greeting cards, duplicates of letters, i.e., returned original and carbon, appointments, and interoffice administrative communications should usually be weeded out and placed in the wastepaper basket. Great care, on the contrary, should be taken to preserve letters or documents which might have legal significance. Whenever material of assorted sizes or weights is involved it is always wise to consider whether it may be copied into the text without loss of value.

FORMS AND OUTLINES

Records are still found in which identifying data, social study, and disposition of the case are all printed headings on a four-page outline, but even in short-contact cases the restrictions of this method seem to outweigh a possible saving of time. The present tendency in the field is to avoid the rigidity of a printed form for the whole record. Outlines for specific topics like health, occupational or home economics studies are used whenever a considerable quantity of classified factual material must be included.

There is a wide divergence among agencies as to the number of forms used. Application blanks, budget schedules, school, health, and placement forms are among the commonest. The practice of making a schematic, diagnostic summary by outline tends to be discontinued. Outlines for social study are less frequently printed on the history sheet than in earlier practice; and if guides are used at all, they are suggestive only and may be kept "under the blotter" for reference rather than for pattern. As a training in formal social study, outlines have a value. It is always a temptation to fill in forms whether the material sought is pertinent or not. At one period workers were encouraged to get all the information possible and place it in the record on the chance that later some of it might prove to be significant. A complete reaction against this resulted in the assumption that to get facts about a person implied that if the worker could find out enough about an individual, this worker would be in a position "to do something for him or to him or with him"—all equally deplored.[4] Such a disclaimer of all personal and social responsibility is as extreme as the older case work efforts to order the affairs of men from without. It is true, however, that the case records of the last five years have become much less schematic and structural as if in response to a case work technique more controlled but less organized and organizing. It is probably also true that as skill in diagnostic thinking has increased, reliance on schedules and outlines for either history or analysis has lessened. In "unit" hospital or court records or any in which technicians make entries one is likely to find a high incidence of graphs, forms, and schedules. This is because of the need for arbitrary restriction of departmental contributions, convenience in finding specialized reports, and the necessities of

---

[4] For discussion of the apparent conflict between the *theme* of social responsibility and self-direction and *therapy* see Reynolds, Bertha, "Between Client and Community," in *Smith College Studies,* 1934.

comparable data when instruments of precision are used.

Indexing of a case is approached in several ways. Formal topical headings in an arranged social study have been quite common as also the main divisions of a record, such as Application, Referral, Social History, Diagnostic Summary, Follow-up, Treatment Evaluation, and Closing Entry. More minute indexing is of two main kinds: (*a*) index to *contacts* either summarized on a special sheet or by marginal headings, e.g., "visit to home," "visit Mrs. Smith," "Mr. H. at office"; (*b*) index to *contents*, "May's health problem," "stealing episode," "attitude toward mother." Most indexing is so poorly done as to have little value, but if writers with a clear sense of significance should index the chief themes it would no doubt add to readability, especially in records following a largely chronological pattern.

III

THE CHRONOLOGICAL ENTRY AND THE SUMMARY

THE oldest forms of case record available may be compared to diaries or accounts of the steps taken by the case worker and events reported in an informal style. However, even in these early case records one comes across an occasional summary and condensation of action taken or of events over a long period of time. The content was of objective facts and happenings since impressions, especially when conveyed through the lavish use of adjectives, were discouraged. Mary Richmond, a great reader of case records, always used to say that she preferred the "open structure," i.e., diary type, of record because she could see everything for herself. Entries of this type have changed little over the past thirty years, and indeed they are probably still the most common. Compare, for instance, the following similar pairs of entries more than twenty years apart.

Dec. 19, '08.—Visited school and saw teacher and principal Acton . . . Mrs. Babbit said at first B was very troublesome, would pout and sulk and sometimes scream at top of lungs when crossed in any way or when corrected; but that by talking kindly to her and insisting on obedience she had improved very much.[1]

Nov. 3, '33.—The teacher stated to the worker that the girl's difficulty is stealing which she began before her mother's

[1] The above illustration is taken from printed but unpublished case records of the years noted. *Charity Organization Society Bulletin*, Vol. III, Mary E. Richmond, ed. Russell Sage Foundation, 1911 and 1912.

death. She steals only from her own home such things as her father's shirts, cans of fruit, dishes and table linen. She gets on well at school and seems to be no problem there. (From a visiting teacher record.)

Oct. 29, '07.—Mrs. Dutton called at the office, makes very favorable report of B. Says she is capable and willing, is saving her money and spends it in a sensible way; the other day bought pair of rubbers for self . . . Agreement is that B shall have $1.50 per week . . . Mrs. Dutton feels she understands B and says she needs affection.[2]

Sept. 2, '31.—Mr. Smith called at the office to make final arrangements for camp for Willie. He made the necessary deposit of $5 and got from us list of clothing. He showed interest and concern that everything should be properly attended to. He asked worker to come and see his wife as soon as possible to tell her about the sewing class as he thinks she needs an interest since her mother's death. (From a child placing record.)

Although the decade 1920-1930 saw a rapid development in the use of the partially or wholly summarized record,[3] some agencies never departed far from chronological recording, permitting themselves at the most a "diagnostic" summary; and even when monthly summaries were used, these appeared as condensed narratives rather than topical rearrangements. The "diagnostic summary" was in fact a form of recapitulated social history. The practice had been to record the social study as-it-happened, or diary fashion, and at some later point in the record, if needed, repeat this material in summary.[4] When the reason for making the

[2] *Ibid.*

[3] "Case Studies" No. 1, Judge Baker Foundation, 1922-1923.

[4] There appears to be some confusion as to the nature of a "summary." Mrs. Sheffield uses the term as meaning "a brief account containing the sum or substance of a fuller account." Mrs. Bristol in her *Handbook on Social Case Recording*, page 168, uses the term similarly—"the periodic summary . . . is simply the summary of material previously recorded between certain dates . . ." On the other hand, Dr. Southard in *The Kingdom of Evils*, page 537, says: "In the discussions of social workers there

summary was a report to a psychological clinic, the headings showed the influence of this purpose.

The commonest summaries are the social history; periodic summary; closing entry; transfer summary (which is like a closing entry in purpose and content, but should be fuller, since the case remains active); diagnostic summary (a form midway between the social history and the diagnostic statement); treatment evaluation and the case abstract (which is for staff or class discussions or states the gist of another case record for incorporation into the current record).

THE SOCIAL HISTORY

The question as to whether to use a chronological style or a blocked topical arrangement arises first with the material of social study. As we have indicated the earlier records were of a diary type throughout for both study and treatment, and this form is still the most common. However, as diagnostic thinking sharpened and the focus changed from the mere reporting of facts and events with the worker's action almost invisible, to a conscious attempt to show treatment, whether of an active executive or "relationship" type, the whole record tended to assume more structure. The pros and cons of "thinking with a schedule"[5] will always be de-

---

seems to be an uncertainty of opinion as to the nature and uses of a summary. Some look to it for a full presentation of the case, a complete digest of the history, which is recorded elsewhere in the form of interviews and letters. We conceive the summary as the briefest possible statement of the essential facts of the case, following in form the outline used for collecting the data. The judgment of the worker in selecting the essential facts necessarily enters into the summary." The writer has used the term to cover not only the summary of material previously recorded but also unrecorded material of study or treatment such as social workers may keep in case notebooks with the purpose of later condensation for the record.

[5] See Richard C. Cabot, *Social Work*, Houghton Mifflin, 1919, p. 37.

bated. Most workers are helped at some period of their training by the use of an outline; in practice many workers will choose to organize all the material in a difficult case for analysis. Few and perhaps no good workers rely on outlines or schedules for either practice or recording. A social history may be prepared in lieu of day-by-day entries from the social worker's notes; it may follow entries such as a summary for the reader's use or for presentation at staff conference or for a report to another agency.

Outlines for social case study summaries have occasionally been published.[6] Thus formally presented the history deals with Family, Home Setting, Neighborhood and Group Life, Occupation, Education, Leisure Time Activities, Health, Income and Resources, Cultural Background, etc. The content of social histories has varied according to current preoccupations and disciplines of case workers. The second decade of the century brought much stress on health histories which were often separated by means of sheets of different colors. At first the family and relatives received attention as resources; later also as influences. The twenties saw the emergence of an emphasis on content traceable to the psycho-genetic emphasis in the child guidance movement. Writers reported on grandparents and the life of the client including birth and weaning experiences. During the same period not only the social experience, objectively described, but also the meaning of it to the individual was sought for. During this period, however, the recording tended to block the client's reactions

---

[6] See Appendix for *Mental Hygiene and Social Work*, Lee and Kenworthy, The Commonwealth Fund; and also *Social Case Work, Generic and Specific* (Milford Conference), American Association of Social Workers, 1929.

under a heading: "Attitudes Towards—Marriage, Parents, Siblings," the case work of the time being markedly centered in the family, with parental relations the dominant note. By the end of this decade, when the meaning of the experience to the client was reaching its peak of professional stress, so much "attitude" was involved that it could no longer be contained in paragraphs, and the record flowed back into a "stream of consciousness" recital such as will be discussed in a later chapter. But on the whole, this was the period when in many quarters the record, especially in teaching and research institutions, was structuralized. The situation as presented by the client was disposed of in a short initial paragraph followed by four or five pages of carefully arranged history, supplemented by medical and psychological studies. This in turn was followed by diagnostic findings, statement, or discussion before treatment was entered.

There is little doubt that interpretation and diagnosis improved markedly during this period and that the recording reflected an attempt to get to the bottom of things. It was hoped that behavior and circumstances could be improved by penetrating the psychological "causes" and by "removing" them. As in other periods of swing, case work seemed to move rapidly and to gain in sureness of touch. Unfortunately the security gained from these long histories and detailed analyses was somewhat illusory, since the case worker could make little use of the material elicited by pressure methods, which often also left the client irritated or confused. A full social study is too cumbersome to illustrate. Not infrequently such a study would run to seven or eight pages, single spaced. Before the depression, however, there had set in a reaction in favor of studying the problem which the client wanted treated, the social study was related to the problem, and with this change came recognition of the significance of "feeling" in more fundamental terms than "attitude."

With the depression the period of leisurely study was suddenly over. What was the good of a full history which no one, least of all the client, could use? Social study and the reported history became alike selective as case loads jumped, doubled, and tripled over night. Case recording became a series of hasty notes in the emergency relief agencies, and in the family agencies the specific need only could be covered. The one historical topic retained, at least in the early years of the depression, was a work history. The practical day-to-day situation became the theme to be considered, with room for little else. Thorough social history, for the most part, was lost in immediacy, but at the same time unique opportunity was afforded for developing the selective trend already in evidence.

Few people would dispute the opinion that whenever a considerable mass of social data is collected it is better to compose an orderly summary than to struggle through the confusion of trying to piece together a picture from day-to-day entries. The cost of records is twofold, and the time cost of reading is heavier than the time cost of writing. If the social data are fragmentary, if the acute situation only is being handled, or if the worker-client interview is being featured, the social study should be recorded in diary form.

Some agencies have never completely abandoned the day-by-day entries for any form of summarized study except for "diagnostic summary" which might be found well along in the record in certain long or difficult cases. During the nineteen thirties there has been in fact a re-emphasis on the chronological method which so extends the meaning of "chronological" that a new description has to be found. Within the day-by-day entry the natural sequence of the study and treatment is now revealed, not merely in cursive entries, but also in such a way as to show process. The recording of process as well as the various forms of summaries in common use are discussed in later chapters. Whether one adopts a structural method, separating study, diagnosis, and treatment, or begins at the first entry interweaving study and treatment, depends in part on whether conditions in one's agency require a somewhat arbitrary period of social study (for example, investigation before parole) or whether one is free to let the client work out his own problem at his own pace and in his own way. In the latter situation formal arrangement and summary are less relevant. One must not forget that in reality case work is a moving, dynamic, shapeless set of relationships, but that recording is an arbitrary rendering. There may be some natural correspondence between the case work emphasis and the style of recording, but this is probably adventitious and not essential. The writer believes that the type of case work does not determine, though it may suggest, a particular type of recording.

It is hard to discuss the pros and cons of summarized histories without becoming involved in a discussion of the pros and cons of obtaining social history. Most case workers would agree that the technique of getting relevant and useful history from an adult about himself is difficult. Under questioning persons may give a history in such a way that further treatment is blocked. On the other hand, plunging into treatment without the guide of history may be inadvisable. Getting history from a reliable adult about a child presents less difficulties, and to get the immediate history of a practical situation is usually a sensible procedure. The point for recording is, that if the emphasis is on "the helping process"[7] that is, worker-client relationship, there is likely to be selection of material, but little arrangement of, and certainly no display of, historical material as such; whereas, if the emphasis is on the life experience there is likely to be more analysis and arrangement of history.

Two entries, giving the opening and reopening of the same case by the same agency six years apart, show the different approach of topical summary and an early step in the recording of process.

INTAKE INTERVIEW[8]
Topical Influence, 1926

Woman's First Husband.—Mrs. M arrived in the U. S. in May, 1905, and in July of the same year met and was later married to her first husband, John Price. Mr. Price, an American by birth, was a man of splendid principles, highly intelligent and successful in his work. At one time, he was a mechanical engineer, but later went into the hardware business, where he made fairly good money. The couple maintained a quite prosperous business on Delaware Avenue and later on Spencer Avenue. Mrs. M assisted her husband in the store and was therefore able to employ a servant for the manual work in her home. They bought little furniture, but such purchases as they made were of the best. It had been their ambition eventually to own a comfortable home. In 1918, Mr. P was stricken ill suddenly and died soon after. With his insurance and a small amount of savings, the widow managed nicely.

[7] See footnote, page 13.
[8] All identifying data in this and following records have been removed.

Woman's Second Husband.—In 1920 Mrs. M met Mr. M, her second husband, through her cousin. He is four years her junior but seemed thoroughly likeable and reliable. In retrospect Mrs. M believes that her cousin through jealousy of her former prosperity brought the two together, knowing Mr. M's real character and realizing that it would mean an unhappy life with possible failure for his wife. The couple moved to Pennsylvania where Mary was born in 1922. While Mrs. M's savings lasted, the marital relationship was fairly happy, but with these exhausted and in fact squandered, Mr. M's attitude became increasingly difficult. The months prior to Mary's birth stand out as the most unhappy experience of Mrs. M's life with the constant quarreling, scenes, etc. At the time of confinement, the mother was seriously ill in St. Olaf's Hospital and three months after the baby's birth was obliged to return for treatment of an abscessed breast. During this period, Mr. M showed no sympathy and has never displayed any real affection for his daughter.

In December 1924, conditions having become so acute, Mrs. M decided to leave her husband. With only a small amount of money, she went to Washington and here attempted to maintain herself by sewing.

·   ·   ·

Same Case, 1932

Mrs. M then talked about her first husband whom she described as a good man and who died in spite of all she could do for him. She told of the success they had had together in running a hardware and house-furnishing store, first on Delaware Avenue and later on Spencer Avenue. She described his illness and how she had done everything she could to make him live, even going to Baltimore to consult Dr. Wise, one of the best known specialists there. She said that although they had been advised that he could never be cured, with good care he might be able to live even longer than his wife. His illness was due to enlargement of the liver. She bent all her energies toward having him live, then said that one day he came home feeling ill and asked for stimulant. Mrs. M talked faster as she described how she had gone from one place to another to secure this for him but could not get it, and after a week of the flu he died. For two years she was a widow until she met the "beast." She talked with considerable animation and her eyes flashed in an angry manner. "That was a terrible experience. I hate to remember it and it is a long story, but I've got to go on." She explained that her second cousin introduced Mr. M to her. She said that he was "all sugar" before she married him; that she had been lonely as a widow and had at one time fainted when she was by herself. She felt that she needed someone with her. She understood that his grandmother had been her grandmother's sister and since he was related in this way, she felt safe in marrying him. She then went on to say that it was not until after she was married to him that she discovered that he was a loafer and commenced to hear people gossip about him. Her cousin never explained why she did not tell her of his shortcomings before. She feels that the cousin was jealous because of her prosperity and wished to ruin her life. She showed great resentment as she told of her husband's indifference towards her when she was ill. When she was three months pregnant, she was suffering with unbearable pain for a week before he would get any help for her. When he finally consulted her uncle concerning her condition, it was Thanksgiving Day. She made a special point of the fact that it was on this day that she had to be operated for tumor. She stressed his laziness and the fact that it was her home in which they were living. The fact that he suggested that she go out and pick up wood seemed to be a threat to her self-respect as she told this with great indignation. Then she told of an incident when he had been at a friend's house playing cards. They told him that if he did not go home early, his wife would be waiting for him with a rolling pin. His retort was, "Well, then I'll not go home," and he sat down to play cards. She went on in a disgusted tone that if he had been a man at all, he would have stood up for himself and returned home instead of staying out all that night as he did. She told of his habits which she considers lazy—his not working but spending the day chatting with friends or going fishing. She explained the fact of his being ambitionless by saying that he would not even take out his citizenship papers until she made him. When she was first married, even though people talked about him, she felt that she would make a man of him in spite of it all and she said she could have done so if there had been anything there to work with. "But he was even dumber than an animal." "He was like a snake—if you picked up its head, it would bite you

and if you took it by the tail, it would go away from you."
In explaining how she endeavored to help him, she said that
when people gossiped about him, she stood up for him and
when they told of bills he had not paid, she said, "He is my
husband and if he owes anything, present the bill to me."
She said that she had had "hope in her heart" that when the
baby came he would change. Her eyes brightened as she explained that as soon as the baby could creep, she had taught
it to go for his slippers and take them to him. This was of
no avail. He showed no affection for the child and became
more brutal to her, going after her with a razor one time. He
showed no sympathy at all for her when she could not work
and as soon as the child was four months old, she went out
again to see what she could earn. She told of his leaving the
home once and of taking him back for a week on the insistence of the baby's godmother though she declared at the time
that she knew she could not change him. She explained that
he was the kind of man who would never make any progress
and he is probably now playing ball or fishing with his friends,
depending on someone to keep him going. She explained that
she always tried to get a step above her present position and
that she was willing to work for it. She recalled at the time
when she was too ill to do anything, her husband had just let
things slip. They had received a dispossess and the furniture
had to be put into storage. Then they went to live in a room
of a cousin's cousin. She said she stood it for as long as she
could and then insisted that he get a home for her and the
child. She clinched her hands and said tremulously, "I wanted
a home for my baby." He did nothing but slapped her on the
face, so a friend found a small apartment for $15 a month.
She said it was dirty and dilapidated but she did not care so
long as she could make a home of it. She said in spite of
everything, up until this time she had never been discouraged
though she had often been provoked. As for her husband she
said, "He was a closed book which I did not wish to open.
God will punish him but I am going my way as I have for
the past 8 years." She has never seen her cousins or any of
her connections in Pennsylvania and expressed the wish that
the "State would burn up every trace of them."

In the second illustration "process" is shown only in
the sense that in the woman's handling of the story her

own approach is indicated. In more complete recording of "process" the worker's approach is also shown (see Chapter VI). In fact, in the recording of "process," treatment process is what is usually meant.

PERIODIC SUMMARIES[9]

Many agencies utilize monthly or three-month summaries of facts, events, and treatment while the family is under care. All cases of a routine or repetitive type and most executive treatment, that is, the mobilizing of community resources, lend themselves readily to summary. Since much case work is of a practical nature, summaries are time saving and answer the purpose quite well enough. Long periods of supervision, as in child care, without active episodes lend themselves easily to summary. Periodic summaries are illustrated on pages 108 to 114. A typical monthly summary in lieu of four chronological entries is the following:

MONTHLY SUMMARY

During the month of October Mrs. X was seen on 10/3, 10/6, and 10/24. Mr. X was seen on 10/9. Our interviews

[9] Dr. Southard at the Psychopathic Hospital in Boston at one time required a topical summary under the divisions of social, physical, and mental history, and the results of treatment were summarized every three months thereafter. "We conceive," he said, "the summary as the briefest possible statement of the essential facts of the case following in form the outline used for collecting the data. . . . A thorough consideration of a case cannot be based upon the summary alone. . . . One of the chief difficulties in studying methods and results in social treatment is the lack of information in the record concerning the plans and purposes of the social worker. It is usually impossible to form any idea of what the patient owes to social care and what to 'nature.' The technique of treatment can rarely be discovered from the record . . . One way of supplying this deficiency is to record at the beginning of the 'treatment record' the general plan that is to be followed and to indicate in the *periodical* summaries of results the modifications of the plan later adopted."—Southard and Jarrett, *The Kingdom of Evils*, The Macmillan Company, 1922.

with Mrs. X were quite short. She was still feeling somewhat weak from the confinement. At the times she was away from home she would leave Mr. X to take care of the baby. We do not know whether she was actually interested in getting back to the child as soon as possible. She gave an impression of being tired, and was apparently finding it quite difficult to adjust to taking care of the baby. It was a drain on her. She felt that after a while when she was more used to it and when the baby was a little older, she wouldn't find it so difficult, but at present taking care of the house and taking care of the child was a hard thing for her to do. We discussed that with her, agreeing that it was a difficult period of adjustment for her to be making at present. Although Mrs. X seems pleased at having the baby, at the same time she seems discouraged over the amount of work that it involves, and over the fact that Mr. X seems unable to get employment. She does not blame him for being unemployed. She showed a good deal of consideration in talking about his feelings. She said that he was dissatisfied and impatient because of the difficulty of finding a job, and that he was upset because they were not able to buy the things that they really wanted. His dissatisfaction seems to center around this and it is most evident when they go out for a walk and he sees a great many clothes and other things that he feels are necessary, but which they cannot get at present. We were able to obtain a few things for them but not very much in the way of clothes.

Sometimes summaries are made at the point of transfer. Such summaries are akin to the closing entry. If made to cover the time between two under-care periods, the entry is called "interval history." Periodic summaries focus on facts, events, and course of treatment. If the treatment is being analyzed, weighed, or otherwise featured, the summary may be referred to as treatment evaluation, rather than periodic summary (see Chapter IV). Transfer Summaries usually emphasize course of treatment and may include some evaluation of the same.

TRANSFER SUMMARY

The J family were referred to the office by a visit from the daughter Gracie in January, 1927, who came because a friend had told her that this organization helped poor people. The family is Greek, living in a poor tenement in the fur district, and consists of Henry and Elsie, about 34 years old, and four living children: Gracie aged 16, Alice aged 9, Lucille 6, and Peter 5.

The father and mother were born in Greece. Paternal grandfather was a doctor, and the father was the fourth of seven children. He received little education. He knew Mrs. J from childhood, as she was the youngest of four children of a poor widow who lived next door to Mr. J's family. Her father worked in the soil, and she had no schooling. They were married in Greece, where Gracie was born, but were glad to come to the U. S. at the suggestion of Mr. J's brother in 1914, because of hard living conditions in Greece. The marriage was apparently a happy one, and they got along all right although Mr. J held various jobs, never earning more than about $18 a week. They have had ten children altogether, but five died in infancy and one was a miscarriage. Mrs. J has never learned English but is a good housekeeper and interested in the care of children.

In 1926 Mr. J became "queer." On recommendation of a doctor he was sent to a city hospital and later transferred to the state hospital. In January, 1927, he was repatriated to Sparta with a diagnosis of general paralysis, cerebral form. Since then the mother has done irregular work in fur and clothing but is unable to meet the situation of providing adequately for the family. For two years she has suffered from a pain in her right side, and recently her condition has grown continuously worse so that she has really felt very ill, but has continued to work and tried to do her best for the family. Her Wassermann was negative, but syphilitic history seems significant.

Gracie is working in a biscuit factory where she receives $15 a week, but the work is irregular. She has a plus four Wassermann for which she is receiving treatment at St. Benedict's Hospital. The younger children have negative Wassermanns but are kept under observation at the St. Benedict's Skin Clinic, and Alice has a bad recurring eye condition. To date the society has confined its treatment largely to health measures. Physical, dental, and eye examinations and clinical care have been given, fresh air holidays and advice on diet and hours. Gracie's income is at present the only one, and she has to attend continuation school one hour a week because the Board of Education reported that she was working illegally, but they have adjusted the hours to suit her work. There seem to be no sources of financial aid which the family are concealing; Mrs. J has borrowed considerably from one of her relatives, but cannot get any more, and there seem to be no others who can help.

To obtain a pension for the family there must be a guarantee that the husband is insane and confined in an institution. A letter was obtained from Athens saying that he had arrived there and was in an institution, but there must be further supervision provided. It is necessary that someone agree to keep in touch with the institution and report back if he is removed from institutional care. In other respects, apparently, the family are eligible for a pension.

Another illustration showing more personality element displays about the same procedures.

TRANSFER SUMMARY

These seven-year-old twins were referred to the clinic by the public school. During their three years in school, in kindergarten, and in the primary grades, William had made excellent progress and was regarded as a very bright child, but Mollie had made practically no progress and was a source of worry to her parents as well as her teachers. Our initial investigation revealed that the parents had no unusual anxiety over the boy, but the little girl's lack of school accomplishment, especially when compared with her brother's, was becoming an increasingly serious problem to them. The result of the psychological examination given Mollie by the Institute in September showed her I Q to be 78. William's examination, given at the clinic's request, gave his I Q as 138.

The twins are the only children in the family, the first child having lived only a few hours. Mr. P is a painter employed by the Board of Education, and although he is now working only three days a week, they have additional income from property so that they have no acute financial worries. There has been no significant illness or mental difficulty in either the maternal or paternal family with the exception of one of Mr. P's sisters, who was slow in school, but who was successful in a stenographic job prior to her marriage. All of his brothers have had some college training, and one is a commercial artist who owns his business. The mother's family are in the laboring class but none of them has had any undue difficulty. Mr. P is of German descent, an alert, wiry person with the German respect for scholarly attainments. Mrs. P is a slow, heavy-set woman, obviously dependent on her husband, but an excellent housewife and mother whose sole interest is in the activities of her family. There is strong family feeling both in the immediate group and among the relatives, most of whom live close by.

William and Mollie are both healthy, friendly children and give every evidence of being well adjusted in the home. Their parents are interested participants in their activities, they follow a normal routine and are treated as responsible members of the household. Beyond the fact that they were Caesarean babies, there has been nothing unusual in their physical development. The difference in their personalities was apparent when they were babies. William was active when only a few months old, while Mollie was willing to lie quietly and made no outcry when her brother finished his bottle and took hers. Her teething period was from two to three months later than William's, and she was about six months later in walking and talking. But her slowness and retaining of babyish ways did not alarm her parents until she started to school.

When the children were referred to the clinic, Mollie had no playmates and was dependent on William or her mother, although William had started to play with other boys and was making an effort to break away. But at home or with strangers he assumed a paternal, explanatory manner toward Mollie. She was beginning to be conscious of her difference from the other children in school and felt badly because "the other kids won't play with me," but the satisfactions at home and her understanding teacher probably helped to avoid any deep feeling of unhappiness. William was making an excellent record in school, was already showing signs of leadership ability, and the only evidence of any difficulty which he displayed was an occasional enuresis.

Treatment consisted in helping the parents to understand the differences in personality of the two children and to recognize and accept the fact that while William had superior intellectual ability which should be fostered, Mollie would always probably be much slower mentally, but that she had also many abilities which should be developed, and that they should not make an issue of her school accomplishment. We made the suggestion that since this particular public school has no ungraded class, they should consider placing Mollie in a special school next fall, if necessary paying a tuition fee. Both parents accepted the idea that William would need money for college training, but that Mollie in order to remain a well balanced child needs special school training during these years, and that money spent for this special training was as important as for William's college. We discouraged comparison of the children and advised that they regard their differences as quite natural in order that neither child should become unduly conscious of his inferiority or superiority. They had already received medical advice concerning William's enuresis, and we gave them some supplemental suggestions, and at the time of the last home call he had not had any trouble for over a month. During the treatment period Mollie has gradually taken more pleasure in active outdoor play and is now playing with other little girls in the neighborhood.

These two illustrations are pointed for transfer and are not unlike closing entries. Periodic summaries may be managed this way or may be rearranged under headings. The choice of one arrangement or another would depend in part on whether interviews, which are inevitably fluid and formless, were being condensed, or whether parts of planned and active social treatment of a specific character were involved.

CLOSING ENTRIES

One of the oldest types of summary is the so-called "closing entry." This may run from the simple statement, "man at work" or "family moved," a mere note as to the disposition of the case, to a short conventional form covering the following points: situation at intake and persons involved; problems emerging; services offered and treatment given; progress of case while under care; results obtained and status on closing. Sometimes significant events in the life of the family are included, and sometimes a forecast in the event of reopening is added. The closing entry should not focus on social study material or on diagnosis, although outstanding problems should be mentioned, but on the course and results of treatment. We are interested, that is to say, in accounting for the progress of the client while under our care. The place for long evaluations of treatment is, likewise, not at closing, unless the case is particularly interesting for research purposes or likely to be reopened. Although administratively a full closing entry is useful in making reports to inquiring agencies, the number of cases reopened is too small to warrant detailed closings. Both diagnostic and treatment summaries should be made so far as possible while the case is active. A closing entry need not in simple cases be longer than a paragraph or so, and a narrative style similar to that given above seems to be the most satisfactory. Although again pressure loads make for neglect of closing entries, most people agree that the brief analysis of stewardship is an important professional self-supervisory tool. Summaries used as reports to other agencies are discussed in the chapter on letters.

CLOSING ENTRY

Mrs. W and five children, ranging in ages from four to fifteen, were referred in September, 1928, for assistance following the imprisonment of Mr. W on a charge of larceny.

Until the time of Mr. W's imprisonment, the family had enjoyed middle-class standards from Mr. W's earnings as a boss painter. Mr. W, partly because of his ambitions for his family and partly because of his sport-loving nature became involved in a bootlegging venture which led him to Chicago. A controversy over the finances with a prospective customer resulted in a charge of larceny. Evidence against Mr. W was not clearly established, but he was sentenced to a minimum of four years. The family's resources were exhausted in legal proceedings. Mrs. W attempted to make her own adjustment by obtaining a janitorial job and by Goldie's leaving school.

The family was found unprepared for the sudden change, as they had been dependent for decisions and for necessities upon Mr. W who, although a domineering individual, was an indulgent husband and parent. Mr. W was considered a pleasure-loving, easy-going individual, while Mrs. W was found to be a dull person whose interests were limited to her household duties. The necessity of assuming the rôle of head of the family and the continued adaptation to lowered standards were accompanied in Mrs. W by neurotic symptoms and increased dependency. Goldie, and Isaac also, showed an indecisiveness and inability to plan or meet their responsibilities. Edwin and Sadie presented minor behavior problems, probably as a result of Mrs. W's state of mind and her lack of knowledge of child care. Grace made a normal adjustment.

Classification of problems: broken home; imprisonment; dependent attitudes; vocational maladjustment; and insufficient income.

Financial assistance was granted during the entire contact, the amount varying with the earnings and attitude of the children. More suitable work was suggested for Mrs. W who, however, showed inertia in finding such work. She continued her complaints concerning "nervousness" and was given medical care. She was unresponsive to an attempt to interpret her symptoms to her, and her dependency showed evidence of becoming aggravated.

Vocational guidance recommendations were made for the children. Goldie, however, made her own work adjustment in clerking. Isaac, who left school on his own volition, did not follow the plan of continuing in trade school, and found a poorly paying job at which he could make no progress. He showed no interest, however, in changing his job, but instead indicated a desire to wait until his father returned. Vocational guidance recommendations were also made for

Grace, who continued to make a normal and progressive adjustment. Country care was provided for the younger children. An attempt was made to interpret the children's problems to Mrs. W, but she refused to allow Edwin to attend a play school.

Mr. W was returned on parole in March, 1931, suffering from a hernia and in need of dental care. He underwent an operation and a program of dental care was instituted. He reacted to the lowered standards in the family with demands on the agency. His attitude we accepted as an expression of a feeling of guilt toward the family. He was encouraged in making his own adjustment. He experienced difficulty in finding work as a painter and was given a small amount with which to buy his own tools. He finally obtained work and moved to better quarters, but requested a continued allowance, which was refused.

The family has become economically self-maintaining. Contact with the agency over a period of two years had produced no noticeable changes in the attitude of the family towards the solution of their problems. Mr. W has probably resumed his old rôle of directing the family. Further contact with the family will probably not yield constructive results. Case closed 9/3/31.

This closing entry shows case work of an executive and counseling sort with goals clearly marked. Its chief fault is its length. Closing entries evolving from cases in which relationship has been stressed are likely to be more tentative, but the fundamental structure is not necessarily dissimilar. The kind of material given in the second paragraph (history prior to agency care) can usually be omitted. A shorter and simpler closing entry is the following:

CLOSING ENTRY

Mrs. M applied for assistance on 3-3-35, having been referred by the ERA. She was ineligible to receive assistance from that agency because she did not meet their residence requirements. She was old enough for an old age assistance grant but could not get proof of her age or residence. There was an acute financial need, since she had exhausted all the resources that she had had after her husband's death. Her chief concern was to try to secure damages and subsequent royalties from a cotton cleaning process invented and patented by her husband, which was being used illegally by numerous cotton concerns. She appeared to be a very intelligent but slightly eccentric old lady, highly suspicious and very active.

Three main lines of treatment have been followed: Financial relief was given to her in the form of rent only, since she said her friends would provide food. She seemed to have a feeling of security in this and to understand that she could always request other assistance if she needed it. Much time was spent in trying to learn something of the legal problem concerning the cotton cleaning process. An effort was made to evaluate her prospects of receiving financial return and to inquire into the standing of the lawyers and interested parties assisting her in this litigation. There seems to be little question that she has a real case and at the present time the indications are that Mr. Kenny, who is working directly with her, is an honest and intelligent person and can be relied upon to guide her wisely. Considering that the possibility of financial returns from the patent appeared very indefinite and hazy, it seemed advisable to help her in making a plan for regular support. She was referred to the Division of Old Age, and help was given her in establishing her age and residence. She was granted assistance from that agency amounting to $33.00 monthly on 3-1-37.

Now that it is felt she has competent advice and guidance regarding her patent affairs and is assured of a regular source of income until such time as she may secure some returns from the patent, there seems to be no further need for service on the part of this agency.

Date closed 3/31/37.

TREATMENT EVALUATION

Treatment evaluation summaries are, as a type, more akin to diagnostic thinking than to case abstracts. Originally the only treatment summary to be found in records was in the closing entry, and that contained happenings and events rather than planned treatment and technique. In difficult or interesting cases or in cases carried for a long time, workers try to analyze and evaluate the treatment earlier than in the closing entry. In the example given below the first paragraph in narrative style seems more flexible than the parts indicated under numerical points. Both parts could have been done the same way; it is a matter of taste. Treatment evaluation summaries usually go beyond the point of describing the course of treatment, which is all that is necessary in a closing entry, to a discussion of the minutiae of technique, weighing successful as well as unsuccessful steps and attempting to account for relative improvement or lack of improvement. A treatment evaluation summary reviews the problem situation in terms of attempts at solution and usually concludes with a fresh plan or renewed attempts along the lines of an old plan. Among case workers who theoretically disavow "planning," formal summaries of history and treatment evaluation summaries are little used. The following shows definite plans and treatment steps:

TREATMENT EVALUATION SUMMARY

Howard is the illegitimate son of a woman who had been cast out by her father for disobedience and who took refuge with a sister and brutal brother-in-law. In this household Howard lived until he was about three years old, when the mother married an inferior man, and they went to live in very poor surroundings. However, Howard found complete security in the positive libidinal satisfaction given him by his mother, and made a good adjustment in school until his mother died, when he was eleven. Deprived of his only security and neglected by the stepfather so that he used to go to school dirty and underfed, Howard began to truant. The case was taken up by the S P C C, and Howard was finally adopted by a maternal aunt and her husband. They had been antagonistic to his mother previously and expected the boy to be grateful for their kindness, while they expected of him a rigid kind of obedience to which he was unaccustomed and deprived him of any independence. Howard, not finding security with them, became unresponsive and at times sullen, resentful of criticism, evasive and silent about his own affairs. His adjustment in school continued to be fairly good, but his marks were not always what his uncle desired, and his attitude at home was so irritating that he was reported to the society. The uncle was at first rather upset because he felt the society was criticizing his method with the boy, but responded when assured that his kindness toward Howard was appreciated.[10]

Mr. S has been given some insight into the reasons for Howard's behavior, and he understands to some extent the seriousness of the boy's previous deprivation.

He has been helped to identify himself with Howard instead of identifying the boy with his younger brother, of whom Mr. S was jealous. This has been done by letting him see many similarities in his own boyhood and Howard's, and by showing him what ambitions he had given the boy since Howard came to live with them.

An attempt was made to get him to give Howard more independence, and Mr. S sees to some extent that he ought to be allowed to make his own decisions. He has not yet been willing to give him an allowance.

Since Howard seemed so anxious to continue his education, and since this was his only source of security, Mr. S was persuaded to allow him to remain in school. Howard is doing better in school, and Mr. S is pleased with his improvement. Howard has been taking the medicine prescribed by the doctor.

The coöperation of the Big Brothers has been enlisted with the idea that when Mr. S comes to them for advice, they will be familiar with the society's plan of treatment and help Howard's progress.

Howard's relations at home seem happier, and he is more talkative and responsive.

Mr. S has not been willing to give Howard an allowance. He is still insistent about an exact hour of coming in at night and does not yet fully understand why Howard should have any feeling about his own father.

[10] It is not usually necessary to repeat history as in this paragraph. A sentence should have been enough. This is repetition of historical and diagnostic material already available in the record.

Reasons for Success and Failure

In so far as Mr. S can identify himself with Howard, it is possible for him to see his need of independence, since he himself left home at such an early age.

Because he has a feeling of superiority to Howard's step-father, it is possible to make him realize the boy's early deprivation.

The fact that he has been given some ego security in regard to his own success and also to Howard's improvement since he came to the S home has made him willing to accept some suggestions and advice.

His ego need is so great that he is not able to entirely relinquish his domination of the boy. He feels also that he should be able to compensate to Howard for any early lacks.

Plan

1. Continue glandular medication.

2. Give Howard a feeling of achievement by commendation of his good school work and his job.

3. Continue contact with psychiatrist to give Howard an opportunity to talk over things that trouble him.

4. Show Mr. S what his interest is and praise Howard's school work. This will give the boy a feeling of self-respect and develop Mr. S's interest in allowing Howard to take vocational training when he finishes junior high.

5. Continue to explain Howard's behavior in terms of his early deprivation and not as antagonism to them.

6. Help Mr. S to identify himself with Howard in every way which will lead to a more understanding attitude in regard to the boy's needs.

7. Give Mr. S suggestions of ways in which he can develop Howard's independence, such as giving him an allowance, trying thus to tie up with Mr. S's desire that Howard shall grow up to be a good business man.

For further illustrations of the treatment evaluation summary see Chapter IV.

Some people would say that chronological, as-it-happened, recording shows treatment method far better than summary and that periodic summaries make for rigidity. The proponents of summary argue that summarizing itself is a discipline in analysis; that day-by-day recording burdens the record with unselected material, much of it of doubtful value; that the practice of holding dictation until a sense of unity and direction can be elicited from the stream of experience makes for significant content. Considerations include such minor points as the facts that if summary is used sources of material should be clearly indicated and if dictation is delayed for any length of time rough notes must be kept either in a day book or loose in the record so that nothing important will be overlooked during the absence of the worker or a change of workers.

Probably most writers would agree on the following points: that both diary and summary are useful, that the selection of one or the other depends on the objectives and general characteristics of the study and treatment and on the size of the case load. In case loads in which services are highly diversified and cases are active for only a month or so, diary entries are undoubtedly easier and more convenient. In critical periods of contact especially if the agency is taking responsibility for what happens, diary entries, kept up to date, are a professional protection if things go wrong. Courts[11] have a preference for diary entries as more evidential, but most social workers claim privileged communication and protection against subpoena for case records. Case records in all fields present social, not legal, evidence.

Single interviews or series of interviews on a "ther-

[11] Many disabled soldiers claiming compensation for injury long after the war were able to offer contemporaneous entries from Red Cross records which established their claims.

apy" or relationship basis are hard to reproduce through any medium, but since it is extremely difficult to indicate feeling except through conversation and behavior, most workers attempt reproduction rather than summary—another possibility being a highly diagnostic method of writing, discussed in a later chapter. In agencies doing a considerable amount of student training or having untrained workers, diary entries for both study and treatment are encouraged by supervisors. If trained workers are employed, eligibility procedures and other procedures calling for definite factual and circumstantial material may appropriately be found summarized and analyzed. A few supervisors think the discipline in analysis afforded by summary is a good reason for teaching it early to students but for self-study and especially for supervision full diary entries are commoner in training centers. We should distinguish case analyses of already recorded material submitted by students, from summaries of original material made in lieu of diary case notes. Case analyses are a routine exercise for beginning workers, and are useful tools in difficult problems.

If a factual and relatively complete social study is gathered it is preferable to have the material arranged and condensed. In case loads with a series of routine entries, such as efforts at mobilizing resources, periods of supervision, or handling of allowances, such services may be economically and satisfactorily summarized. Health programs and habit training may be arranged and condensed for the record. Condensation may be achieved either by abstract, or by abridgment through selection or deletion, or may be effected by rearrangement into topics. In straight abridgment, marginal index headings may be used with good effect.

To recapitulate: the commonest forms of summary are those of the social study; the periodic summary (which may or may not substitute for the text itself and tends to include facts and events of social significance as well as problem and treatment;) the treatment evaluation (which stresses the movement or progress while under care;) and the closing entry (which is a case abstract in miniature but focused on the course of treatment, particularly noting results obtained.) The distinctions made here are somewhat arbitrary. Summaries are, in fact, made whenever convenient and necessary. If the workers are not highly trained they tend to recapitulate facts and events only. If the workers are trained in social case thinking summaries will be selective; now featuring facts and events and behavior in the study process, now interpretation, now treatment evaluation, now results obtained, or combining these in various degrees for a case digest, short or long, analyzed and diagnostic or factual, depending on the use to which the summary will be put. Long, academic case analyses prepared for classroom or staff conference have not been illustrated. We must remind ourselves of the limitations inherent in summary—the tendency towards over-simplification, towards sharp outlines when the life process is fluid and shapeless, the danger of obscuring sequences, and possibly of blurring the emotional overtones in human behavior. Sources should be indicated in study summaries and care should be taken to bring out reactions to treatment in treatment summaries. Since treatment is begun and trends may be established whenever a contact is made, a service rendered or an interview held, many workers dislike summaries which make for a segmental handling of the material and prefer to reveal process through straight narrative. Balance should be retained between material which lends itself readily to summary and that which does not. A long chronological record becomes unreadable unless supported by summaries at suitable places. The so-called diagnostic summary, which, in evolution, lies midway between social history summaries and purely interpretive statements, will be discussed in the next chapter.

IV

INTERPRETATION OR DIAGNOSIS AND PLAN OF TREATMENT

THE ordinary treatment record is inherently problem solving or diagnostic. Whether the client uses us for his needs or whether we are engaged in active steps taken with him or even for him, the case record is more like a play or a novel than a literary essay. It has focus, theme, climax, movement. The patient comes to us because he is suffering from something in his life relationships. With Dr. Adolf Meyer, therefore, we put "the complaint in the center of our interest because it is in the center of the interest of the patient." Whether we think of a social situation or choose to weight the "relationship" elements and so interpret them more narrowly as a "client-worker situation," there should be diagnostic insistence and constant evaluation.[1] When the young worker asks if he should record everything because some of the facts may later prove to have significance, we can only point out that it is impossible to make a complete study of a social situation and that just as a feeling for potential significance makes a good diagnostician, so a feeling for potential significance distinguishes a good record. A thorough-going interpretation of a case includes the naming and interrelating of difficulties (social causality) both imme-

---

[1] Sheffield, Ada E., *The Situation As the Unit of Family Case Study,* Social Forces, Vol. IX, June, 1931.

diate and less immediate, the naming and evaluating
of strengths or assets, the classification of outstanding
problems, and the recurrent examination and weighting of treatment factors. The very process of selection
and arrangement of material points to interpretation,
and beyond the diagnostic factor in selection we may
find recorded, formally or informally, impressions, inferences, diagnostic summary, diagnostic statement,
classification of problems, treatment evaluation, diagnostic discussion. The client alone can know the meaning of his own life experience, but the professional case
record is the writer's attempt to express, as practitioner, the meaning of the case. This imposes limitations at once upon the selection of material. The meaning of a case from a research worker's point of view
has enough differentials to warrant separate discussion.

Early case records do not show always a clear distinction between fact and judgment. "She is quick and
clever with her needle . . . There is material for a
good woman in her." "She always has sound judgment
and the gift of seeing through shams," 1906. "Blanche
cried very pitifully but tears are like April showers;
can laugh or cry with ease but still seems to try to do
what is asked of her," 1902. "Is very untruthful, but
is capable—lovely with children and when she is good
is very helpful, but the black moods come pretty often
and then she is very ugly and is just as ungrateful as
can be," 1904. "Family very intelligent, very funny;
mother still crippled with rheumatism but does not
now use crutches," 1908. "The house fairly clean but
Mrs. O was untidy; plain to be seen that she is a drinking woman," 1912.[2]

---

[2] "Case History Series," *Charity Organization Society Bulletin*, 1911.

Today case work would be able to go a little deeper than "black mood" and would be less moralistic and less emotional in its analysis of behavior. Case records show more objective language in diagnosis, and the place of diagnosis is given more dignity and emphasis. Students and beginning workers frequently show some degree of subjectivity in their attempts at interpretation. The use of adjectives and adverbs generally reveals more about the attitudes of the interpreter than about the factors in the case. As understanding of behavior, relationships, and social situations grows, case workers become able to make significant inferences with less personal bias, and we call these disciplined professional inferences diagnostic thinking. If we attempt to follow diagnostic practices decade by decade in a general sort of way, we shall be able to indicate several phases in the evolution of the "meaning" of a case.

The practice in many family agencies, from 1910 to 1920, approximately, was to bring the difficult cases before a committee. The worker would present the facts orally and give some interpretation. The committee would discuss the implications of the case and then give a decision embodying "the plan" which would be formally entered on the record. The discussion would not appear in the record, but a notation of this type might be found:

11/2/15: Case before Evening Committee for discussion. It was voted to have Mrs. Young go to hospital for confinement; keep up budget system; give advice and friendly visits; watch Mr. Young while his wife is away; gradually lessen supervision.

We can readily see that this represents a plan rather than an interpretation. Early records featured plans and "next steps" rather than an analysis of the problem. These case committee decisions may be contrasted with the diagnostic discussions or staff conferences of which illustrations are given in this chapter.

Record interest at this time centered more on the question as to what was or was not a justifiable inference from a given set of facts than on any attempt to define and interpret a total situation. *Social Diagnosis* gave us a brilliant analysis of social evidence in investigation, but the book as a whole emphasized the processes leading to diagnosis rather than diagnosis itself.[3] "Social diagnosis may be described as the attempt to make as exact a definition as possible of the situation and personality of a human being in some social need —of his situation and personality, that is, in relation to the other human beings upon whom he in any way depends or who depend upon him, and in relation also to the social institutions of his community." ". . . the diagnostician, *who must have had social treatment in view from the very beginning,* has been measuring at every stage of his work the treatment value of each circumstance, each human relation and each personal characteristic." (The italics are ours.) Followers of Miss Richmond promptly forgot the essential limitation in the italicized part of the above sentence. What, said they, shall we include in diagnosis, how much of the situation, how much of past events, how much of the complexity of the social world? The diagnostician is, however, not a social scientist. He has treatment in view at every step thus making for a high degree of selectivity. The form of diagnosis used by Mary Richmond, for

[3] Richmond, Mary E., *Social Diagnosis*, Russell Sage Foundation, 1917, p. 357, *et seq.*

example, The Persons in the Family, Difficulties Defined, Causal Factors, Assets and Liabilities, became the
classic model of diagnosis for years and still may be
found in case records. Phrases rather than whole sentences were preferred, such as: crippled breadwinner
with defective child; illiterate family with no savings—
poverty due largely to alcoholism, and so forth.[4]

About 1925 a classified list of findings, with a corresponding grouping and classifying of services rendered, had a brief vogue. These diagnostic summaries
were often long and the illustration given has been cut
to some extent. We may observe the "active" nature of
the material which strikes the reader as really more
"plan" than diagnosis.

DIAGNOSTIC SUMMARY

Topical influence

Physical.—Mr. Hall. He is in need of treatment for his
teeth which may be causing focal infection, thus intensifying
the neuritis. Mrs. Hall. Her general resistance seems to have
suffered under the severe mental and physical strain. The
older children are in need of tonsillectomies and follow-up.

Economic.—A few debts still remain. The income of Mr.
Hall is insufficient without the supplementary contributions
from Mrs. Hall's salary. The gross income is still far below

---

[4] In 1919 Dr. Cabot (*Social Work,* Houghton Mifflin Co.) was suggesting
to social workers a schedule for diagnosis consisting of four items: The
individual (physical and mental) and his environment (physical and
mental). Although this did not affect the field so generally as did Miss
Richmond's form, occasionally it can be seen in old medical social records.
For years several large family agencies used a schedule in which diagnostic
items were classified under the captions: Health, Economic, Behavior. In
The Kingdom of Evils, The Macmillan Company, 1922, the Southard
classification was: *Morbi, Errores, Vitia, Litigia, Penuriae.*

In 1922 Dr. Healy and Dr. Bronner were using a schedule focused
more on the individual but using phrases rather than sentences. The headings in the published case series were: Problem, Physical, Mental, Background, Possible Direct Causation, Prognosis, and Recommendations.
Judge Baker Foundation, "Case Studies," Series I, 1922.

earlier standard of living. Mrs. Hall does extra work whenever an emergency arises, causing an undue strain.

Social.—The parents are without social outlets; they do not feel in a position to cultivate their former friends. Mollie remains without suitable recreation.

Mental.—The strain under which Mrs. Hall has worked has created an habitual nervous tension which suggests the need of attention until she achieves a sense of security. On the other hand, the danger of over-emphasizing special examinations or other undertakings, which the ordinary intelligent family might reject or those whose value Mrs. Hall does not recognize, must be avoided. Mollie seems to have reacted normally to an abnormal situation. The unconscious responsibilities which have been placed upon her together with a recent possible sex trauma, caused by attempted assault, suggested the desirability of psychiatric study.

Plan

Physical.—Mr. Hall. Further contact for Mr. Hall with the physician who has been giving private service free. Recommendation of a dental clinic at which teeth may receive attention. Mrs. Hall. Make efforts to have mother return for further x-ray and recommended treatment. Watch carefully her physical condition and arrange for relief of strain as it is necessary. Arrange through clinic for tonsillectomies. Plan to have general physical examination for Mollie. Continue contact with nursery to determine health reports and needs of children.

Economic.—The family have managed budget to include the payment of the remaining debts. Watch the increase in Mr. Hall's salary. Work with family toward the time when the mother may stay home and herself train the children. Encourage family in regaining former standards of living as the income permits. Attempt to eliminate home work; discuss this problem in all its aspects with Mr. Hall.

Social.—Discuss establishing pleasant relationship with St. Paul's Church. Ultimate encouragement of the family in regaining entrance to circle of former friends. Provide recreation for Mollie. Arrange for drawing lessons in a preliminary development of her talent. Encourage boys in their Y.M.C.A. adjustments of Boys Club.

Mental.—Establish a closer relationship between father and the society. Continue contact with relatives and convey to them a sense of admiration of the father's achievement. Mrs. Hall. Continue close contact with the mother in order that she may feel a sense of security, not dependency, in her confidence in the society. Discuss problems as they arise with the mother to relieve her feeling of the burden of sole responsibility. Mollie. Arrange complete psychiatric study of Mollie. Appointments for intelligence tests of all the children.

Note in the Hall summary how interpretation tends to be expressed in treatment concepts. Workers beginning to practice diagnosis are apt to say "Client in need of relief," or "Patient in need of a rest cure," rather than to find phrases expressing economic insufficiency or a convalescent disability.

Other categories were experimented with during this period. In the next illustration note under "Problem," the orientation sentence which later became typical in "diagnostic statements." The rest of the material is much more a summary than an interpretation.

DIAGNOSTIC SUMMARY

Problem.—Mrs. S is an Armenian woman, age 27, of low grade mentality, deserted by her husband and determined to keep her children with her although seemingly incompetent to care for them and earn their support. Little of the history of either man or woman has been obtained, nor is the real basis of the marital difficulty known.

Background in Armenia.—Mrs. S was born in Constantinople and was the youngest of four. It is stated that her father was a knife sharpener. There is little indication of Mrs. S's attitude toward either of her parents, or of the status of her family. In Armenia, she apparently suffered the persecutions of her countrymen. The record suggests the possibility of Mrs. S's having belonged to a Turkish harem, but this seems to be based only on visitor's observation of a tattoo mark on Mrs. S's face.

In U. S. With Relationship to Family.—On coming to the

U. S. at the age of 10, she lived in Syracuse with her sister, went to school then, and later worked in a canning factory. At the age of 16 she married Mr. S according to her sister's wishes and apparently against her own will. Mr. S took her immediately away from Syracuse after which Mrs. S's family no longer considered her as one of them but as belonging to her husband. Mrs. S related this fact with tears in her eyes. It is noted, however, that Mrs. S returned to her sister's home for the birth of each child and also at various times during the worst of her marital trouble. In 1923, after six years of marriage, including periodic desertions, it is stated that Mrs. S returned to N. Y. from Syracuse because her family would have nothing more to do with her. It is therefore not known from these factors what is the exact significance of the relationship between Mrs. S and her relatives or the degree of security or insecurity they mean to her.

Mrs. S and Marital Situation.—In regard to the marital situation from Mrs. S's point of view, she maintained at one time that she and her husband were "as happy as most people are." Furthermore, in 1923, after six years of unhappy marriage, Mrs. S denied her husband's desertion. She also said that she liked her husband at first because he was "big and strong." In 1926 she followed him to N. Y. to try to make him support her, and after his desertion in 1927 she took the trouble to follow him up at his brother's. In describing the nature of their unhappiness, she accused Mr. S of drinking, gambling, beating her, and not giving her sufficient money for food. At the time of the birth of the first child they apparently lived apart for some time. When in 1920 Mrs. S filed complaint in court against her husband, she learned for the first time something about Mr. S's early life, such as his place of birth. The court at this time brought about a reconciliation and Mr. and Mrs. S lived together again. In 1923 Mrs. S again took her husband to court, after trouble with her sister. She claimed that while her sister was visiting her home, she found her sister in bed with Mr. S. The court ordered Mr. S to pay $10 a week for support, which he never carried out. After this there is indication of a friendly relationship between Mr. S and his wife's sister.

Mr. S in Relation to the Community.—Accusations against Mr. S from sources other than Mrs. S are his indictments by some of the neighbors. Neighbors on the whole, however, seem to have taken sides in his favor. It is recorded also that Mrs. G considered him "bad" in 1923 and that she had opposed the marriage from the first. On the whole, however, both Mrs. S's relatives, his own relatives, and the neighbors seemed to feel that Mrs. S was at fault instead of her husband. Mr. S's relatives stood by him consistently and often referred to Mr. S's fear of his wife. They felt that Mr. S was fond of his children and said that he frequently gave them presents.

Mr. S in Relation to Family.—Mr. S. apparently assumed some responsibility toward his family and made several efforts to establish a home. In 1925 he expressed his willingness to support his children but refused to live with his wife. He once wanted his sister to take the children and several times expressed his desire to have them placed. He tried to get a divorce but was unwilling to go through with it unless he could have the custody of the children. His interest at this time was apparently not encouraged; in fact, he was scolded for not keeping his promises to pay. Mr. S's outstanding effort to re-establish his home was in 1/27 when he, feeling badly because he had not seen his children, returned to Syracuse where his wife was, had her sign a paper before a lawyer to the effect that she would be a good wife, and brought her back to N. Y. to re-establish his home. When he then found it impossible to live with Mrs. S, he separated from her but made arrangements for her to receive groceries through his brother's store, Mr. S guaranteeing payment of the bill. He stopped this help and disappeared altogether seemingly only after Mrs. S had disgusted him with her scenes in his brother's store.

Mr. S and Marital Situation.—From Mr. S's point of view of the marital situation, in 1920 he accused his wife of physical mistreatment in sexual intercourse and immorality. In 1925 he expressed his feeling that his wife was crazy and repeated in more detail points regarding her physical cruelty. He stated that after each attempt to live with her she was impossible, and in 1923 he changed his job so that he could not be found and forced to go back to his wife. He maintained that she sat on the doorstep refusing to do anything, never made any attempt to do good housekeeping and neglected the children. He also accused her of going to Niagara Falls with another man. It is noted that he followed this accusation with the remark that she soon returned because her friend was tired of her.

Mrs. S in Relation to the Community.—From sources other than Mr. S, Mrs. S seems to appear at fault. In 1923, the neighbors accused her of immorality, begging, and mental disorder. She seems also to have had petty quarrels with her neighbors, although it is recorded that during Mr. S's desertions, Mrs. S was able to live on the kindness of the neighbors. Both Mr. S's relatives and her own relatives as well considered her at fault.

A few years later the diagnostic formulation was breaking away from categories into a more interpretative yet at the same time still somewhat factual picture. We can see the specific items or findings showing through. The emphasis was, all through the twenties, that of antecedent causality.

DIAGNOSTIC SUMMARY
Narrative style

Mr. C, about 41 years of age, a butcher's assistant by trade, is a native of Tipperary, Ireland. He has been living in this country continuously since his marriage in 1911 and has been a periodic drunkard for about the same length of time. The increasing frequency and duration of his sprees have reduced his family to destitution. Mr. C is in a depleted physical condition. He is also in need of dental care, as the condition of his teeth may be a partial cause of his neuritis.

Mr. C, when sober, shows a sensitiveness and reserve which make it difficult to approach him on the subject of the fundamental causes of his drinking. He does not appear to realize that such causes exist, describing each time the event which irritated or discouraged him and which precipitated that particular spree. He acknowledges in confidential moments that it is difficult for him to endure the naggings and recriminations of his wife on the subject of his drinking and shows signs of injured pride if not deferred to as the head of the family. Mr. C has had certain fastidious ideas on living and on personal care which have suffered from the crowded poverty of his home and the poor housekeeping of his wife.

Mrs. C has learned to shoulder the family burden. Her work as janitress reduces the rent from $25 to $10 a month. She earns in addition $8 a week by cleaning. With the assistance of her sister-in-law, the church, and the agency she has been able to keep pretty good control of the financial situation during the four years known to the society. Although an industrious worker, Mrs. C is too unsympathetic and too overworked to be successful in sustaining an atmosphere of order and discipline in the home. She has no outside contacts and no leisure. For this reason she has grown to consider the hours spent away from the house, during which she is cleaning, as recreation. She makes attempts to raise the standards of the home, both in her housekeeping and in the discipline of the children. Mrs. C is entirely wrapped up in her children and will sacrifice herself for what she believes to be their good. She exacts a great deal of help from the two older girls and is uneven in her discipline of them all. She loses her poise under the tension of too prolonged a spree of Mr. C's, denouncing him for his frailty and declaring her intention to leave him, although in calmer moments she has a complete realization of the fact that her affection and understanding for him are such that she could never endure such a separation.

In the twenties case work had taken on a distinctly historical flavor and even in diagnosis "background" was featured in varying degrees. Examples of emphasis on background are found in the preceding chapter. Later, background was worked up into the current situation (Mr. C illustration) although the note of antecedent causality was struck repeatedly in diagnoses of this type.

The early mental hygiene movement, emphasizing the determinism or purposiveness of behavior (cause and effect relationships), with special emphasis on the early developmental years, influenced the diagnoses of this period to evaluate past experiences and come through these up to the present, as shown in the following illustration. We can see that the material here has evolved from the primitive, categorical, factual summary with little diagnostic element into a real interpretation with little factual recapitulation but with the interpretation itself strongly oriented to early life experience.

DIAGNOSTIC SUMMARY

Psychogenetic influence

Problem.—Mrs. B, adoptive stepmother, describes problem as lying, persistent disobedience, and difficulty of management. Inquiry also brought to light some dawdling or day dreaming and masturbation.

Interpretation or Diagnosis.—An interpretation of the patient's behavior involves, it seems, an understanding of the personalities and attitudes of the father, stepmother, and patient, and their interactions on each other.

A complete evaluation of the father is impossible at this time. There are several things that may be noted, though they are somewhat difficult to integrate in the same individual. He describes himself as a "mother's boy," indicating a mother attachment or dependency. Yet he made, at least until his present marriage, what would appear to be a fairly good and balanced ego and libidinal adjustment. The first marriage is described as ideal, though we do not know what rôle he played in it. Since his second marriage, it would appear that he is dominated by his wife and perhaps has slipped back into his old mother dependency. This is not entirely satisfactory to him, it would seem, because he disagrees with his wife about the discipline of the patient, although he allows her to do most of it.

The stepmother identifies herself with her mother, saying that they are as alike as two people can be. She recalls disapproving of her mother's methods when a child, but says that she now approves of the dominance and the sternness of her mother and has modeled herself after her. She seems to be pursuing that pattern in relation to the father and the patient. The mother had had two previous experiences in raising children, her brother, thirteen years younger, and her niece. She admits failure, and the facts would seem to indicate that her method of handling them was somewhat different from the way she handles the patient. She is said to have done everything for them.

First of all, we can see that she is a rival of the patient with the father. We do not know her real feeling for the father, but some indication that her unconscious hatred of the patient may not be so unconscious is given in the statement that she loves the girl but will come to hate her. When the stepmother first took charge of the patient, she may have had a certain ideal goal she wanted to attain, but she states that she was determined to make a successful job of Eleanor and on the first day explained this to her. She pointed out, from the beginning, all the little things in which Eleanor failed.

Essentially the situation for the stepmother would seem to be as follows: She is in a position of rivalry with the memory of the first wife and with the patient in relation to the father. She is jealous of the father's affection for the patient. She rejects the patient and blames her for the lack of harmony between herself and husband. She punishes her husband by pointing out indirectly that his first wife did not raise the patient properly and by blaming the patient's behavior on him. She carries into the situation and perpetuates her mother's dominating and stern methods and is only partially successful in dominating her husband (being stopped where the patient is concerned) and practically unsuccessful as far as the patient is concerned.

In regard to the patient, very little is known about the first seven and one-half years of her life with her mother and father and of her behavior then. Enough is intimated to give the impression that she was thoroughly spoiled and probably used to having her own way. Her father adored her, saw no fault in her, and made much of her tricks. With this kind of experience behind her, one would not expect her to get along well with teachers or students at school. We do not know if this is true when she first went to school, but she does not get along with other pupils in school now.

For an analysis or interpretation of a foster home with a later evaluation of the home in terms of the child's experience there, see Chapter VIII.

Contemporary diagnostic work is considerably diversified. We find variants of the forms given above in many fields and also adaptations of which diagnostic statement and diagnostic conference are perhaps the most important. The phrase "diagnostic statement" was, the writer thinks, first used by Miss Antoinette Cannon in connection with medical social practice. This form is particularly suitable when recording must be as compact as possible, for example, in a unit medical social record, but it is also a good working form for the practitioner with an average case load in which he wants to keep the diagnostic element realistic and the recording not too burdensome. A handful of diagnostic statements from various fields will serve to illustrate this form of interpretation. Diagnostic statements, because of their simplicity, may occur at not infrequent intervals as new problems or new patient foci emerge.

DIAGNOSTIC STATEMENTS

A. Elderly, single, psychotic woman with slight cardiac limitation, who for many years has lived in self-imposed isolation on limited means. She is absorbed in a cause which she feels demands long, irregular hours of labor without compensation. Her refusal to regulate her life as to food and rest and her over-emphasis on her illness and discomfort are an outgrowth of her need for personal sacrifice and attention. *Outlook:* Only slight improvement is to be hoped for. By stressing the necessity of regular meals and by minimizing the importance of the cardiac condition she may be able to gain weight, but whether she can develop peace of mind by this method is more doubtful.

B. A thin, sensitive Polish woman who developed a toxic thyroid following the shock of her husband's death. She worries constantly over the family income which is lowered by her inability to work, and which is uncertain because of the precariousness of her children's jobs. The presence of her aged, senile, mother-in-law in the home is a further source of disturbance. *Outlook:* Real rest is difficult to obtain under the present situation. The economic strain cannot be greatly mitigated, which is likely to retard her progress, although her interests and independence will keep her from too great regression.

C. Case of an American family consisting of a man, 35, his wife, 30, and three school-age boys. The family life is being undermined by drinking habits of the man, with a lowering of standards and under-nourishment of the children ensuing. In addition to the problems of insufficient income, the oldest boy especially is suffering from being identified with his father, is sullen, unresponsive, and has recently joined an extremely undesirable gang where drinking is the main amusement.

D. This is the case of a seven-year-old boy of Austrian-Jewish parentage. He is very much the baby in a family of adults, there being three older children. The emotional environment of this home is extremely unstable. The father is infantile in his outlook, needs praise, petting and encouragement constantly, has no awareness of his children's emotional needs, and takes out his own irritability by finding constant fault with every member of the family. The particular place of quarreling is at the dinner table, and patient found that he was ignored until he adopted unacceptable behavior, such as eating with his fingers and kicking his sister, who sits next to him. In fact, since no attention is paid to them on any basis except a fault-finding one, the only way in which Bert can get attention is by annoying each one of the adults in turn as much as he possibly can. He is making quite a success of this. The taking things and hiding them would seem to worker to be part of the rest of the picture of this desire to annoy parents and sisters as much as possible. It seems impossible, from the mother's statements, that this stealing could be done at night during the sleep-walking. Patient probably denies all knowledge of taking the things or where they are put through defensiveness, for straight through this family lies (as a defense) have been necessary, since such a severe attitude has been taken by both parents. Since patient was a tiny child he has heard stealing discussed, because both George and sister took things from the time they were small well up into late adolescence, and there has been a constant harangue about them and at them about this. How much of a part all this discussion has played in Bert's propensity to follow in their tracks, it is difficult to tell. He has grown steadily more negativistic since the age of three years, so that at present his mother's way of handling him is to request the exact opposite of what she wants.

E. Mr. T's poor health (cardiac disease) on top of his business failures has added to his feeling of inadequacy and has given him many moods of depression. He tends to withdraw more and more into himself, often spending hours alone in his room refusing to see people. Mrs. T, though accustomed to leaning on Mr. T for advice and protection, has reversed her relationship by assuming a protective attitude towards Mr. T and undertaking major responsibility for the family. She finds satisfaction in concentrating her efforts to aid Mr. T toward recovery. She is a wholesome influence in the home by stressing every sign of improvement in Mr. T and taking an active interest in the children. She thus, indirectly, counteracts her mother-in-law's influence without in any way offending her. Both Mr. and Mrs. T's relatives are friendly, but they live at a great distance from the family and have little influence on the family life.[5]

In these illustrations several elements call for comment. In examples A, B, and E we see the idea of outlook or prognosis instead of plan of treatment. The notion of recording a plan is particularly relevant if "executive treatment," or service, is contemplated or if environmental factors are to be manipulated or if habit training or other similar education is to be attempted. Planning is less easy to state if methods of progressive education are to be employed and the client is to learn from experience in a dynamic situation. A formal plan seems less relevant in so-called relationship treatment or attitude therapy. The ideas of treatability, planning, controls and outcome instead of plan are, however, inherent in all methods of treatment and not the least in relationship therapy. If the worker has a

---

[5] In the above the interpretation is obviously on a "situational" or "symptomatic" level which makes it none the less useful.

definite plan it is probably wise to state it; if the plan
is one offered by the client and agreed upon with the
agency, it is wise to state it; if no plan is contemplated,
it is impossible to state it.[6] Workers of certain training
and approach would prefer to think of "movement"
rather than activity, and when the stress is on the
client's use of the worker rather than on the leadership
of the worker, the planning process is fluid and difficult
to formalize in any ordinary sense. A pervasive consciousness of treatability, nevertheless, is characteristic
of these "unplanned" records appearing in connection
with diagnostic discussion, treatment evaluation summaries, processed recording, and even in closing entries.

In sample E, we should notice the anatomy of a
favorable prognosis. Positive or compensating factors
are apparently sufficient to outweigh the liabilities.
In the older records, "liabilities" were placed in one
column and "assets" in another, and workers quite
truly said they could not distinguish problems from
liabilities. There is no way of determining an absolute
value for assets and liabilities, but relative value may
be involved in a contemplated course of treatment.
Are eight children or a mortgaged house assets or liabilities? No one can say. But if we have analyzed a case
so as to give the main configuration of difficulty and
have envisaged a course of treatment, we may, by evaluating the positive and negative factors, give ourselves
some notion as to the likely prognosis. Not even the
most experienced person can be sure of the outcome,
so recording is necessarily guarded, but the intellectual
effort of prognosis is more advanced than is a book-

[6] For a discussion of goals in social case work see Taft, Jessie, *The Dynamics of Therapy in a Controlled Relationship*, p. 18 *et seq.*, 1933.

keeping list of assets and liabilities. Just as diagnosis or interpretation has evolved from simple recapitulation of history, through findings and classification to subtler forms of imaginative insight, so assets and liabilities have been developed from the merely schematic to a clearer sense of treatability and outcome.[7]

Perhaps some simplified examples of various ways of getting at the meaning of a case, using findings, classification and diagnostic statement, may be helpful. First a simple factual breakdown:

FINDINGS[8]

1. Young Greek widow with two children living at home.
2. Exhaustion of insurance and savings leaves them without resources except for relatives.
3. Woman had a hard life of drudgery prior to her happy marriage.
4. Husband died in explosion leaving woman pregnant with second child.
5. Posthumously born child, aged 4, extremely delicate and called for mother's attention from birth.
6. Relatives oppose woman working out of home.
7. Elder child, aged 7, Irene, has temper tantrums, abuses her sister, and is hard to discipline at home and at school. Has I.Q. of 130.
8. Woman is affectionate with children and intelligent. Embroiders beautifully and is eager to learn what she "does to Irene" to make her so bad.

"Findings" are here used instead of full recapitulation; that is, a selection of the most significant factors is listed but not interrelated. The reader must still infer meaning from the selected items.

[7] See also a schematic way of analyzing a case in Dr. Kenworthy's ego-libido chart. Here the value element is described in positive and negative, constructive and destructive terms. Lee and Kenworthy, *Mental Hygiene and Social Work*, The Commonwealth Fund, 1929.

[8] The Findings, Classification and Diagnostic Statement are based on the same case material.

CLASSIFICATION OF PROBLEMS[9]

1. Bereavement; 2. Financial dependency; 3. Sibling rivalry; 4. Over-protected child.

In classification we index only the main problems for research and statistical purposes with no attempt to give the minutiae and subtle differences which make each case unlike every other case. Whenever we want to show how unlike a case is to a type, we must use some sort of diagnostic statement. Whenever we want to show likeness to the type, we must classify.[10] It is not enough to look at happenings in the order in which they take place in human experience; we must also classify things according to their essential nature.

DIAGNOSTIC STATEMENT

This is the case of a Greek widow's child whose temper tantrums and aggressive behavior at home and at school are in part a reaction to an intense rivalry situation with a

[9] See for an attempt at problem classification: Hamilton, Gordon, *A Medical Social Terminology,* Presbyterian Hospital, 1930.

[10] Miss Antoinette Cannon has given us a very good discussion of the case and the class in a recent textbook: "In teaching social case work we must make a distinction between the study of the individual problem and the study of generalized problems. The individual case is the concrete illustration of the general or abstract problem, as for example, Disease, Ignorance, Poverty, Vice, Crime. To say of any case that it is a case of crime is not thereby to have understood the meaning of that case as a whole, nor to know what help or treatment to give. Yet to know something of crime as a general problem is to have something to use in the understanding of the case which presents the clinical picture of crime. Analysis and classification of case problems serve a purpose of research in the field of social case work. For the treatment of the individual case they serve but indirectly as they furnish the means whereby the worker arrives at an understanding or attribution of meaning which would never come with a single unrelated experience. If the student is to learn not to make wrong use of classification in practice he must be taught in such a way as to avoid overemphasis upon general knowledge . . . With growth of interest in the meaning of the whole, prejudices against the classes in which the case belongs subside and the more useful professional attitude emerges."— Cannon and Klein, *Social Case Work;* New York School of Social Work Publications, 1933.

younger sister to whom the mother's attention is constantly directed both because of her delicacy and because she is the last "pledge" of a much loved husband. There are also obscure guilt factors involved. The mother's restricted life and cultural habits keep her within the home circle, and the interest of relatives, although a potential resource, is over-dominating. Exhaustion of savings will soon make the family financially dependent. The mother's manual skill, general intelligence and capacity for insight (she wants to know what she "does to Irene" to make her behave badly rather than what can be done for Irene) and the superior intelligence and vigor of the child herself suggest a favorable outcome.

The diagnostic statement here carries us to a little deeper level than the more factual and historical "findings." The facts are the same, but they are worked into a configuration which inevitably is more trenchant. Note the parenthetical use of "a finding" to support the interpretation. Assets and liabilities could have been indicated through the regrouping of findings, but instead they are here carried into prognosis. Obviously these several suggested forms are academic, since the treatment focus has not been given and the configuration itself would vary as among a request for maintenance for the family, a problem in child guidance, and others. Although case work has gone through a period of emphasizing history for its own sake with inevitable intellectualizing and rigidity, its reaction towards centering on the immediate foreground has other pitfalls. Likewise, in interpretation, we have the dilemma of trying to express our concepts in somewhat general and primitive problem units or else in so comprehensive and qualified a formulation as to be unusable. The important discipline is to state and clarify only those connections that are practically and emotionally vital to the social situation which we are engaged in treating.

A less rounded diagnostic statement, part of a longer summary, will be seen below. Note the informal style and the parenthetic use of findings. A paragraph of this type is often marginally captioned "Impression" or "Interpretation":

During our two year contact with Mr. Conrad, it has been our feeling that he is a profoundly childish individual who leans on his mother, the F.s, the worker, or anyone else who will let him lean. Although a quite hostile person who expects everyone to let him down (he always pushes until he is let down), he thinks of himself as a person who feels nothing but love for his children and his family. Anything unpleasant he always prefers to ignore or put off, in the hope that he will never have to face it. (The F.s, he feels, were responsible for his wife's death, and he knows that they are blaming Bertha for her death, and still he placed Bertha with them.) In relation to any decision that has to be made, he is usually in a completely balanced state of ambivalence. He seems incapable of learning from experience.

The diagnostic discussion differs from the diagnostic statement chiefly in that, being a product of staff conference, it is usually more detailed and more hypotheses are introduced and debated. Yet the thread of diagnosis, proposed treatment or treatability, in spite of the unsymmetrical character of "minutes," can clearly be seen.

The first illustration shows the historical and psychogenetic influence:

DIAGNOSTIC CONFERENCE AND PLAN

Staff conference

Patient is the second son of Jewish parents born in New York City, on 3/17/27. He is the middle one of three children, the eldest of whom is dead. English is usually spoken in the home.

The child is afraid of shadows, will not go to sleep at night unless light is left burning, awakens each evening crying, and cannot tell why he cries, temper tantrums at home and on the street, stubbornness, contrariness, protective lying, imaginative lying, sensitiveness, clinging to mother, nervous, irritable, controls mother.

In the case of this child we know nothing of his inner life. His behavior shows a marked over-dependence on the mother, whom he is able to control quite readily. Whenever he tends to break from his mother's protective grasp, she reaches out to prevent such a move. The mother is obviously the seat of the trouble, and it is to her that we must first turn our attention.

The mother's early life is essentially one of libidinal deprivation. Such affection as she received was from her father, never from her mother. She was not the favorite one in the family, and her education was neglected in favor of that of the older son who was the grandparents' pride and for whose sake they returned to Europe. With the absence of the grandfather, mother appears to have sought and found satisfaction on an ego level in her business relations. Then we find her giving up the work in which she was so successful (according to her own account) in order to have the satisfactions of a home and of a marriage in which the physical side played an important rôle upon a distinctly superficial and conscious level. Moreover, we find her marrying the first man who kept company with her.

It appears that the marriage fails to give the mother all the satisfaction which she had expected. She feels that her husband is not her intellectual and social equal and they have little in common save a satisfactory sex life. The mother has continued her ego drive as a compensatory mechanism and reads, attends lectures, and listens to radio talks on child care. She now wants to realize in her children her own unfulfilled ambitions.

It is not clear to what extent the first child served as a libidinal outlet. The mother describes herself as wrapped up in him, but this may be retroactive falsification. With his death, she passed through an emotional crisis which resulted in transfer to the patient. It may have been due to loss of the love object on which she claims to have centered her reactions. Other factors may have been feelings of guilt over his death and the deprivations due to the simultaneous loss of the home comforts for which she married.

In any event, this crisis seems to have precipitated a marked centering upon the patient as the sole libidinal outlet. The result is a rather typical over-protected child. The mother needs him and is in constant fear of any influence that will wean him away from her. Although she allows him to play on the street, which he appears to do without her, she never permits him to be examined except in her presence, since the examinations are a distinct threat to her.

The father is a somewhat minor factor in the picture. His early life was likewise one of deprivation, but he appears to have achieved much libidinal satisfaction in his marriage. Lacking a strong ego drive, he seems to be content to allow the mother to be the dominant person in the home, and himself to play the minor rôle with respect to the patient.

The mother's fears with respect to the patient may be a transfer as a result of the loss of the brother whom she put in the care of others. The mother must be treated as the patient in this case. The worker must go on the basis of getting considerable transfer first of all. In view of the mother's fear of doctors, the social worker should take the major responsibility. It would be better to make the mother come to us and to take her out of the home, in which she is too tied, if this is possible.

The mother's tendency to project the responsibility upon the patient may indicate that she cannot face reality. She feels the need to be the center of attraction. This doubtless is a factor in her opposition to his being examined alone.

The thumb sucking may be treated by substitution of a number of sucking objects, scattering the habit and eventually eliminating it. The mother must be taught to minimize attention to the habit. With respect to the mother's fear that the patient is imitative rather than imaginative, it must be explained to her that he is at an age when he naturally imitates.

The prognosis in this case is poor. If the mother does not enter into relationship with the worker at an early date, the case should be dropped.

Ultimate goals.—Shift mother from centering on child as satisfaction and interest her in "growing him up." Encourage the mother to build up some of her premarital satisfactions. Turn mother's interests to things which are satisfying to her, but outside her child. Appeal can be made to her on the basis of the child's need to ask questions and her need to have the necessary information to answer him. These goals can only be accomplished to a certain degree on account of the limitations set upon the situation.

Immediate goals.—The social worker will try to obtain rapport with the mother; the patient to be placed in a nursery school or kindergarten in the fall; the father to be encouraged to play a greater part in the patient's life. This to be made acceptable to the mother as a means of helping her.

Major responsibility in this case is with the social worker.

A simpler type of evaluation is the following:

TREATMENT EVALUATION SUMMARY[11]

Treatment during this period was carried on by weekly contacts. The aim was to help Kenneth develop a sense of self-sufficiency, to emancipate him from his mother, and to equip him so as to make an adjustment within the limits of his capacity.

Since it was felt that Kenneth was still in an infantile stage of his emotional development, the worker attempted to develop a boy and girl companionship without encouraging Kenneth to become dependent or to use her as a confidante. Weekly excursions to exhibits, museums, etc., were carried out usually at Kenneth's suggestion and with Kenneth making the arrangements. He kept all of his appointments but was incessantly late. During these trips Kenneth was productive, and as time elapsed he appeared more spontaneous and at ease. It is difficult to evaluate actual progress, but it would seem that Kenneth developed to some degree socially. He joined a social club and went to several parties, which he had not done before. He did not enter into any athletic activity but appeared to have considerable insight into his evasion of this. He assumed initiative to some degree in making plans for his future and decided definitely to go to college and to become a psychologist. Due to financial pressure it seemed that Kenneth would go to evening session and work during the day.

[11] From this summary a paragraph of discussion has been omitted.

Progress was slow, and while Kenneth remained fundamentally childish, he appeared to be weaning himself from
his mother and to be going through the homosexual stage
through contacts with the psychiatrist and one of his teachers.
The purpose of his relationship with worker was to make
transference to a girl of his own age possible. While Kenneth
did not do this he went to several functions where girls were
present and seemed to show greater interest in becoming affili-
ated with coeducational groups.

The treatment evaluation summary, if done periodically, reflecting the judgment of the social worker, is apt
to be less complicated than the treatment evaluation
which reflects a staff discussion. Just as diagnosis may
be in problem form, in diagnostic statement, or in
diagnostic discussion, so treatment summaries may be
simple factual statements, simple periodic evaluations,
or treatment evaluation summary and discussion,
which may include quite minute technical considerations or may be confined to indications as to success of
the general course of treatment. Prognostic material
should be guardedly used, and directions to other workers should be omitted. This is equally true for transfer
summaries, in which the temptation to tell someone
what to do next seems to arise. It is more effective and
in better taste to indicate in the course of treatment
what has been done or not done and let the new worker
draw his own conclusions. Unusual cases suggest excep-
tions, but we are safe in saying that it is generally better
to give clear interpretations of our own work than to
write prescriptions for others.

The next illustration shows an evaluation pointing
towards reasons for closing the case.

TREATMENT EVALUATION SUMMARY

Since the last treatment conference on 7/17/31 the social

worker had four contacts with the mother, two with patient (during which time he was also relisted by pediatrician), and three contacts with the school.

In the light of the case conference decision of 10/22/31, patient was not referred to the endocrine clinic, but re-examined by the pediatrician who performed the recommended re-check on haemoglobin, differential blood count and Wassermann. Both patient and mother were given report of the negative Wassermann at their request.

Patient's complete school record was secured, and all his present teachers interviewed. His record shows that from the time of first entrance to kindergarten in 1922 through the 7B3 grade his conduct was A, B plus, or B. Since that time he has received A, D, and two C's. His class work is marked B and C through 7A with a wide range of numerical ratings since that time.

His teachers report that he is absent a great deal, that he is very poor in academic work but apparently more interested in shop. His present course contains a minimum of academic subjects and a maximum of shop training. He will be graduated in February. In the classes conducted by men teachers he is reported as being an incessant conversationalist; in the classes of dominating women teachers he "just sits." He feels he would like to go to Textile High next term because some of the other boys he knows are going there.

Patient retains his uncommunicative attitude, answering questions in monosyllables with very little free verbalization. He comes to the Institute because his mother insists on it but defeats her purpose by refusing to talk. He gives no explanation of his school absences other than that he plays ball in the schoolyard and doesn't hear the class bell ring. He claims to have a "Y" membership and says he goes swimming sometimes.

The mother continues to identify the patient with his father who has never shared responsibility. She contrasts him unfavorably with siblings and is concerned because he falls below her desires for him. She seems to have been unable to accept any attempt made to interpret the situation to her. She is now worried because she does not know with whom he associates after school hours. She wishes boarding-school placement to prevent further difficulties which might possibly arise through his unfavorable companionships.

An attempt is to be made to ascertain information regarding the possibility of patient's attending a parental school. Mother desires this. Her unfavorable comparison of patient with siblings and her classification of him with father causes him to feel inferior and makes placement away from home advisable.

Early closing is suggested because (a) psychological findings reveal nothing of significance, (b) medical findings reveal nothing treatable, and (c) social case work efforts have revealed an untreatable situation. Mother was not frank with the white workers. She was able to accept the colored worker on a libidinal basis but did not accept her suggestions as she did not continue to put them into effect after the worker left. She is projecting the problem on the agency and seems to be unable to accept any responsibility for it. The loss of her father upon whom she leaned for solution of her problems caused her to feel inadequate and to reject treatment of the patient in the home. Father is out of the home the greater part of the time because of his long and irregular hours of employment. Boarding school where patient could have male teachers (father substitutes) who could give him the ego ideal he lacks will probably effect the most satisfactory social adjustment which can be seen at present.

The following illustrations show the same type of discussion, but the content reveals the different emphasis of a later case-work period.

DIAGNOSTIC DISCUSSION

Case conference

Interviews with Jack[12]

We ask ourselves what are the problems here. There is fantasy of a kind usually characteristic of the ten-year-old child. The fantasy gives us some picture of the client's feeling, i.e., hostility to the parents; possible rejection of the mother person. From it and the general nature of the narrative we gain the impression of a boy, immature emotionally, physically,

---

[12] Discussion here is related to an interview series rather than to the case as a whole. Also the reporting of discussion smooths out any clear cut lines between study and treatment or between treatment and the evaluation of treatment steps.

and intellectually. The content is difficult to follow. We would be at greater advantage if we had more factual knowledge in respect to the neighborhood setting and mores. We wonder to what degree this boy's guilt is resolved by the fact that he is in league with other associates against adults; how much security he gains because his hostility is that of the group. Is this his way of protecting himself against parents and parent substitutes?

With respect to the interview we might ask ourselves first whether focusing of the discussion would have been preferable to the methods we used, that of allowing the client to lead, we following throughout; or second, if, for the sake of building further contact, it was better to allow the client free range. In clarifying our feeling here, we might bear in mind the fact that referrals are frequently made to us on occasions when the anxiety is known at the moment to be painful for the client; and again when there is no anxiety. The referral in this instance is ambiguous. The crisis for the boy is, in a sense, past. We have no way of knowing the degree of anxiety he feels over the present situation.

In order to deal constructively with this area of the unknown, we need to consider what our approach may mean to the client. The child, in particular, may test the worker out. She, to him, may be the symbol of a hostile world. He may lapse into passivity because he is afraid of her. He may keep her on a surface basis of relationship by talking of superficialities as, for example, camp, recreation, etc. The worker can fall into the dangers of snatching at this chance for contact. She may avoid the issues by letting the discussion remain on this level. Sometimes she may try to keep it more on the basis of adult interests and so question the child about school. In neither instance does she allay anxiety if it is present. Actually, she may increase it. The child has no way of telling when she is going to "strike." The challenge to the worker is one of knowing how to allay anxiety. One way of doing it in this situation might have been to have helped the client to tell us why he has come. We cannot expect him to declare his purpose in a very articulate way or to define his problems verbally, but it may afford the worker an opportunity of letting the child know what her interest is. It is her opportunity to introduce herself and to give him a chance first to talk and to help him to dispose of most urgent anxieties.

It would seem possible that we had a chance to do this very thing in this case and fairly soon after the first interview started with Jack. Following the passage (Page 2B) "Jack said that would be fine and sat back in his chair. A pause ensued."—we might have used this opportunity to have made some much comment as "We know boys have trouble at home and of other kinds also. If they want to talk to us about them, we'd like to hear and then see what we could do to help. We know that boys sometimes haven't anyone to talk to." We would make use of the impersonal "boys" here because the client talks in terms of his group. We need to learn when to interrupt so as to allay anxiety; so as to relieve the client's fear of us. We can try to set the stage in terms of our interest in the child and in our interest in the possibility that he has problems. One of our goals would be to help him approach his actual problems and to talk spontaneously about them.

The challenge lies in our not allowing our treatment to remain on that level if we have reason to believe there are more fundamental problems. In cases where there appears to be a relationship difficulty, where the client pushes the relationship toward the worker, worker would need to try to go beyond that. In other words, she would talk about the concrete service in addition to the other.

Unless we succeed in establishing a basis of service other than that of the concrete, what can we hope to do after the particular service is completed? Perhaps if the client really wants the worker badly enough, he will find other excuses to call on her but with the danger that relationship will not get beyond the superficial level.

This boy's fantasy has a different coloring from that we often see. There is a form of fantasy which to the client becomes more real because he thinks the worker is going to accept it as reality. There is that form also, in which the client's need is not so great for an audience. It would seem the latter manifestation in this situation.

It might be advisable for us soon to see Mrs. M. Possibly her handicap is not as severe as we were led at first to suppose. We have tended perhaps too completely to efface her. We cannot see her while Jack is at camp, but later, if contact is resumed with him, we may find it desirable to talk with Mrs M. Perhaps we would do this at first only by attempting to draw her into the conversation when and if she calls at the office with Jack.

Another illustration shows an interpretation of the case as a whole.

DIAGNOSTIC DISCUSSION[13]

Case conference

This case presents a young woman with two illegitimate children who finds herself dependent upon her parents for shelter and upon the agency for maintenance. The acknowledged father of the children has detached himself from the picture, evading the responsibility of the mother's or children's care.

Mrs. W shows many positive qualities—in the love of her children, her wish to keep and maintain a home, acceptance of responsibility. She performs the functions of motherhood, giving the children loving care. She shows a degree of initiative. She has a good work record and plans to work for her own support as soon as she is able.

Significant Behavior of Mrs. W.—Mrs. W evidences a great deal of hostility toward the people who constitute her world. Mr. and Mrs. W, Senior, waste their money on liquor and neglect her. Mr. W is "no good," "stingy," and "a bum," and she does not like his family. The hospital is neglectful. She laughs at the nurses who make spectacles of themselves because they have been drinking. She rejects the new baby. She was reluctant to arrange medical care for herself and for him and apparently had attempted an abortion. She expresses death wishes for herself and for the child. Before his birth, she wished that she dared give him to Mr. W's mother to rear. In her prompt acceptance of the idea of placement of Charles "at the place on —— Street" she was unconsciously rejecting him.

She is anxious to punish those who have hurt her. She considers taking Mr. W to court. At another point she suggests that she will move to his neighborhood with the children where Mr. W's friends would see and pity them, because Mr. W would "hate that more than anything." When she was

[13] An intermixture of findings, interpretation, and comment. Note the brief diagnostic statement—hardly more than a title—which introduces the discussion.

angry with Mrs. W for not allowing her brother Frank to go to camp, she took the money from her mother and told him to go.

There is ambivalence in her feeling as Mrs. W brings out the love she holds for her family. She speaks of her parents as being nice when they are sober. They are good to her and to Pete; she gets some satisfaction from their caring for her. She named the new baby after his two grandfathers. She is bringing out her positive feeling for Mr. W increasingly. She is jealous of his relationship with other women. Although she discusses for some time the possibility of taking Mr. W to court, she does not go through with it. She speaks of a friend who "felt like two cents" when she faced her husband in court. She wishes that Mr. W would talk things over. When he comes to the house she asks him why he does not "do right by me and get married" (5-14). She speaks of their having been happy together in their own home. The picture of this is fragmentary and may be fantasy. She wished Mr. W had come to the hospital at Charles's birth, having had him with her at the first baby's birth apparently meant a great deal to her. Behind Mrs. W's strong positive feeling for Frank, there is identification with him—both had the same bad parents and the same difficult environment. She enjoys her children and feels sorry for them because they have so little.

We may suppose that Mrs. W's evident wish for marriage is in part because of the status it would give by its stamp of respectability as well as for love and companionship. Her secretiveness and self-protection is also partly a result of her ego needs. She states that her children are to be "none of his." However, her insistence that she would marry only for the sake of the children shows her inability to admit her positive feelings. Guilt over her relationship with Mr. W is the motivating force in her reserve in all her contacts. Her need for work and drive to secure it, arises in part from guilt, as well as from initiative and a wish for independence.

Treatment Evaluation.—We have endeavored to enable Mrs. W to bring out her positive as well as negative feelings toward Mr. W. Contact grows very slowly—it is hampered by our possession of confidential information which she is not able to bring out. We should have been able to clear this up sooner. Difficulty in seeing the priest was an obstacle. Anxiety on the worker's part is a factor as shown in our inquiry several times about the adequacy of her diet, and at times too lengthy discussion of this before the question of her marriage had been discussed. Our handling of Mrs. W's mother's drunkenness is better, and she is enabled to express a good deal of her hostility without "upsetting" us and thus increasing her guilt. As contact continues Mrs. W becomes increasingly free and apparently finds some release in the relationship. Despite the strain under which she lives, she continues to meet her situation in a mature way. We assist in making medical arrangements with other agencies.

Outlook.—We shall coöperate with Mrs. W in her plan to work and establish a home for herself. We shall keep in close touch with the situation in the home of her parents, and if the strain of staying there becomes too great before Mrs. W is financially able to leave, we can assist her in moving to rooms of her own near a nursery where the children can be cared for. We are aware of the dangers of the situation—the possibility of creating dependence, and the possibility that Mrs. W will again accept her husband without his assuming any responsibility. We want to see Mr. W although we would not want to insist upon his coming. Hopefully, through our contact with Mrs. W he can be brought to want to come. At this point it is impossible to say what Mrs. W's final decision regarding Mr. W will be, but we would be glad if she should decide to marry him because of her obvious positive feeling for him and because the status marriage would bring would mean so much to her as well as to the children.

Occasionally technical evaluations are related to a single interview. The example below illustrates such an attempt. Discretion suggests the sparing use of treatment commentary which may easily degenerate into *apologia.* The most appropriate setting for technical criticism is that of records specially built up for study purposes.

TREATMENT EVALUATION

Technical comment

5-26-37: Mother brings patient for appointment. Dr. Y is unable to be here on this date, but again mother follows worker into the interviewing room and settles down for a visit, although seeming to find it difficult to say anything. She asks about the doctor, feels sorry he is ill and hopes he can come back soon. There are a few desultory remarks about the weather (mother speaks of the heat making her feel very badly) and then she mentions that possibly the family may go to Rhode Island for the week-end . . . (content of interview omitted)

. . . After a particularly long silence, worker's anxiety causes her to say that mother may feel free to go if she wishes. We enjoy visiting with her, but have felt a little disturbed that mother has been twice disappointed in not having patient's interview with psychiatrist materialize. Despite this, it is significant that mother neither makes any move to go nor replies to the remark. She waits a minute and then says that of course she knew about the children when she married and so was prepared to "make the sacrifice." A few more minutes elapse before mother says that she had always thought of being a children's nurse as a job she would favor . . . (content of interview omitted)

. . . In this interview, because of mother's lack of effect, which has been striking in all the contacts thus far, and because her responses seemed so slow as to be almost painful, worker wondered if she was forcing mother's attention and continued presence by her activity in making efforts to keep the conversation going. Worker's expression of this anxiety on her own part was an error which probably failed to do much damage only because mother's need to express herself was much stronger than her inability to be articulate indicated. Actually mother seemed unconscious of our interruption. It is as if the conflict but dimly expressed outwardly dominated the situation and kept her there in spite of worker. Note that mother stayed over the hour and that for the first time (this being our fourth interview with her) mother tried to bring out material related to her own problems and adjustments. The material was brief, scattered and not verbalized as a problem, but offers the first clues to mother's insecurity in the situation.

For discussion and illustration of diagnosis as interpretation to the client rather than of the case see Chapters VI and VII. Interpretation in this sense is, we believe, to be regarded as treatment and is not the formulation of interpretation for the record as we have been considering it in the examples given.

Evaluation lies close to diagnosis, but we think of it more in connection with treatment. What has proved better or worse, more or less constructive in the progressive handling? The norms in evaluation are social and personal. Mores shift from generation to generation and from country to country, and people may differ or deviate markedly from the mores without necessarily feeling unadjusted. The case worker has to resist alike the temptation to arbitrary over-simplification and useless qualification. "This seems apparently, in a manner of speaking, to be approximately something or other." All diagnostic effort or treatment evaluation is extraordinarily complicated, tentative, and flexible, and is understood as such by the well-trained reader or writer of records. The difficulty is not in recording clearly but in learning to think clearly, and no record can be said to be professional until our fragmentary and imperfect diagnostic thinking is included. The patient exposed to the full battery of scientific method was right in complaining that he wished just for once he could be treated for what ailed him.[14]

[14] A different approach to understanding or diagnosis has been fully developed in the new *Journal of Social Work Process*, Pennsylvania School of Social Work, Vol. I, No. 1. As Miss Dawley expresses it in her paper on "Diagnosis," page 26 of this journal: "Case work diagnosis lies in this area of clarification of exactly what a person is asking of an agency, discussion with him of what the agency has to offer and the way in which it can be offered and determining with him whether this is what he wants and is ready to take at this time. Diagnosis in its deepest and most profound sense, in social case work, is an understanding of what is going on directly between the client and me, as a representative of the agency, in this new experience he has sought." The recording implications of this point of view would seem to the writer to be chiefly emphasis on the "process" style of recording and a free interplay of diagnostic comment.

In summing up we may say that the diagnostic habit is more important than any form it may take, and that diagnosis has evolved from the factual summary through schematic forms to direct interrelation and interpretive formulation. The simplest types of working diagnoses seem to be: the diagnostic statement which defines the case and classification which indexes the problems for statistics and research. Other expressions of diagnosis are found in case analyses for educational purposes and case discussions or diagnostic conferences. Simpler expressions are found in parenthetical or marginal impressions or comments so labeled. Well-founded inferences from substantial factual material are part of ordinary professional writing and need no headings. The professional record as a whole tends to be diagnostic, while the social science document is less focused on treatment and is more consistently or quantitatively factual. This is not because the professional record shows less respect for fact but because the treatment objective sharpens selectivity from the outset and insists that the meaning of the case shall be elicited from the observations made.

V

LETTERS AND REPORTS

THE place of letters in social case work is strategic. Letters are an important part of interpreting one's function to the professional and lay community. Omitting letters to raise money or acknowledge contributions and all letters which chiefly serve administrative purposes, our main consideration will be with inter-agency letters. Social case work in America has not yet been clearly functionalized and clients are likely to experience several agency contacts in the course of relatively short periods. The problem of interchange, of coöperation and interpretation of diverse courses of treatment, is a real one. If agencies are housed in the same building or if the professional group is closely enough knit to rely on the informal conference or the telephone, written reports are less necessary. But in many cases letters must be written, inevitably so in out-of-town inquiries and preferably as a matter of reference in other situations.

Like early diagnostic summaries, early letters were a recapitulation of most of the facts in the case often followed by a long list of specific questions. Emphasis was on fact-gathering and fact-sharing. Conscientious workers in response to agency and community inquiries patiently wrote out long case histories, then added briefly what had been done for the client and, since inquiries were frequently about the least socially competent among the clientele, added the usual depressing results, without a single shred of interpretation to mitigate the story. The courage and intellectual honesty of the writers one can only admire; the effects of this thoroughgoing procedure may, from a community point of view, have given case work a hard reputation to live down. Even if the family under conscientious ministrations did not by some happy intervention of Providence come to a sad end, the picture was flat and matter-of-fact. To reconstruct one such is to reconstruct fifty of this type.

The Smith family came to us in June, 1918, asking for assistance. At that time the family were living in such and such a place, appeared to be such and such type of people, had such and such children born to them, developed such and such illnesses, and showed such and such behavior. Case was closed for lack of coöperation.

Early letters not only offered circumstantial material instead of problem and treatment but also, unfortunately, prescriptions as to what the second agency should do.

We are interested in Ruth Red, age 19, an unmarried mother, living at 338 Forbes Avenue. Her former home was in Y and her parents are dead. (A paragraph of history follows.) May we ask for verification of the girl's story, and will you telegraph us, collect, the result of your investigation. We shall be most grateful for your help in this matter. We particularly wish to know (1) who paid for her fare from P to W last April, (2) whether the Burns Davis family are willing to receive her and, (3) what Burns says about the question of paternity.

Very truly yours,

To say merely that we are interested in a case is to give the other agency no real point of intersection, whereas to state the situation and what we are doing about it is immediately referable to the correspondent's purposes.

The first observation made by any reader is that many letters should not have been written at all. They are a waste of anyone's time. It is still far too common for someone in Agency A to sit down and write a letter to Agency B in Baltimore or Topeka or Dallas asking that agency to take the trouble to find out something which Agency A, by a little time and patience, could find out from the client himself. There are occasions when putative fathers or deserting husbands or the parents of runaway children have to be communicated with through a third party, and there are emergencies of every kind which justify a hasty letter while one is attempting to understand the situation with which one is confronted. But in general we should caution ourselves to be sure that our own treatment position and purposes are clear before a letter is undertaken. Otherwise one seems to suggest that Agency B is merely an accessory to Agency A's purposes.

As between two professional agencies we can assume that the problem itself is sufficiently stimulating, and that social agencies do not need to be cajoled or motivated or urged to coöperate if the inquiry lies in the appropriate area. But if the mission is difficult, the distance great, or the agency unused to the service requested, the writer will do well to consider the ordinary frailties of human nature and supply the correspondent with a reasonable interest motivation and add such courtesies as make the service easier. The State Hospital which once wrote to a family agency something as follows had not only an inadequate sense of professional function but very little knowledge of human nature.

Dear Madam: John Smith, a patient in our hospital left a straw suitcase at 16 West Colorado Street and also left a brown overcoat with large lapels in the Grand Union Terminal. Please forward both to us and we will gladly pay the expenses.

A more persuasive letter is of this type:

Director of Social Service   Re: Tommy S.
St. Matthew's Hospital   Yr. number 26537
New York City

Dear Miss Blank:

We have at present under our care the family of John S, unemployed, his wife and three children, the youngest of whom, Tommy, was born in your hospital. Although we have been putting in an allowance of nearly $30 a week and giving dietary supervision, Tommy, aged two, is losing weight, cries, and is fretful constantly. Would you like to have him brought back to your clinic or would you advise us what steps to take? Mrs. S seems a chronically over-anxious person. Would anything in your experience with her and the children throw any light on her attitude, especially on her overprotection of Tommy?

Very sincerely yours,

In this letter, although there is a long case history, only such facts are selected as bear on Tommy's problem. Notice also the proper assumption that the hospital will be interested in a former patient. Some harassed writers say that from institutions and other agencies, no matter how well composed the letter, a routine response is all one seems to obtain. This is doubtless true, but we must also remember that letters, even in the best agencies, have only recently begun seriously to give interpretation and selected facts instead of unreadable blocks of material. With the growth of professional content, both in diagnosis and treatment, there has been an observable shift toward focusing the letter on the treatment and selecting such findings as seem to bear on this treatment focus or are likely to bear on the treatment focus of the corresponding agency.

The medical social field began quite early to attempt interpretation of the medical social problem in their inter-agency contacts. The following letter shows the present medical social situation, relevant history selected with some reference to the medical problem, what treatment the medical agency gave, and what area of participation is desired from the correspondent.

February 11, 1927

Mr. John Williams, Secretary
The Charities
Worth Street
Boston, Mass.   Re: Peter V
                        Chart Number: 627534
                        Address: 16 Eastern Place
                        Brookline, Massachusetts

Dear Sir:

The following is a summary of our medical and social history of Peter V whom we referred to you for assistance January 26, 1927.

Mr. V has been under the care of this hospital since December 3, 1925, for Exophthalmic Goiter and Hyperthyroidism with accompanying heart damage. He was operated on the first time for partial removal of the thyroid in January, 1926. Following this operation he was boarded for the necessary interval of convalescence at the home of a Mrs. S and readmitted to the hospital for a second operation February 8.

After his discharge on March 24, he was again boarded with Mrs. S for further prolonged convalescence. He started to work as elevator operator in June and was able to continue at work until November 19. At that time he broke down again, and a three-week rest was recommended by his surgeon.

This was financed by an allowance from our convalescent fund.

Mr. V is now classed as a II B cardiac, and for the past six weeks has been trying to find suitable employment. The doctor feels that he would be able to take an elevator position if it does not involve too much strain, i.e., handling of traveling bags or freight, such as is sometimes required in hotels. His condition is expected to improve slowly with his weekly treatments in the Skin Clinic and radio-therapy every three weeks. If these do not prove effective, however, he may need another operation later. In any case, the doctors expect good results eventually.

The social service department of this hospital has paid for convalescence at a total cost of $213.65. We have no general maintenance fund for outpatients, and Mr. V is now able to take a suitable position if one can be found. It is particularly important for a thyroid patient to be as free as possible from anxiety, as emotional disturbance and worry hinder his successful treatment.

Mr. V tells us that he was born in Porto Rico in March, 1888. He finished grammar school there and left home at the age of 17 years, going first to Portugal, then Cuba and finally to Boston nineteen years ago. Mr. V had been in business for himself, first as a cleaner, then as a taxi driver, and finally as a salesman of Victor records. He was successful in a moderate way for several years, at one time having $900 savings which he claims to have lost. He was found to have an illegitimate daughter, now aged 7. Three years ago through his lawyer he started proceedings in the Probation Court to obtain the custody of this child. At the same time he became involved in a lawsuit in connection with damage to his taxi cab. He seems to have become emotionally upset by these lawsuits, and decided to escape to Boston. It is interesting that he dates the onset of his physical disturbance from this time. Mr. V has a mother, two sisters, and two married brothers in Porto Rico, whom he saw last six years ago and with whom he corresponds. He says that they know of his illness, and he is certain that they are unable to help him with money.

On his arrival in Boston, Mr. V did "odd jobs" until he was forced to come to the hospital. Since then he has found work through the Bureau for the Handicapped as elevator operator. Mr. V has been a most coöperative patient. He has kept appointments faithfully and always seemed to do his best to follow the suggestions of the doctors and social workers. He seems to have made few friends in Boston, perhaps due to his ill health and need of rest.

We will appreciate any help which you can give him, as in his present condition he needs to be spared too much exertion and strain. We will be glad to give you any further information which we may have and to make any suggestions regarding the needs of his physical handicap.

Very sincerely yours,
Director of Social Service

The amount of history included makes the letter somewhat heavy. In the following exchange of letters between a hospital and family agency, history has been largely subordinated to a shared treatment relationship.

Mr. John Smith, Director   January 11, 1935
Public Welfare Department Re: Emil S
           No. 44988-A
           2638 Monte Ave.

My dear Mr. . . .

As you know Mr. S was in the hospital from December 6 to December 18 for a hernia operation. This was not performed because of patient's heart condition, which is due to high blood pressure. When he reported to Cardiac Clinic on January 9 he complained of headaches and his blood pressure was still rather high. The doctor ordered an electrocardiogram, which was taken on January 10, and which showed some recent changes in the coronary arteries, which may interfere somewhat with the blood supply to the heart.

It is therefore imperative at this time that the patient have complete bed rest for a period of two weeks and avoid all worry and excitement. Arrangements have been made for a visiting nurse to call in the home daily, and patient is to return to clinic on January 31, at which time another heart test will be taken and patient will be again seen in Cardiac Clinic. We have communicated with the family regarding these recommendations.

We would appreciate having a report from you regarding patient's sleeping arrangements and facilities for rest and care in the home. May we have this report before his return appointment?

Sincerely yours,
Director of Social Service

Superintendent   January 23, 1935
St. Michael's Hospital   Re: Emil S
                                             No. 44988-A
                                             2638 Monte Avenue

My dear . . .

In reply to your letter of January 11, 1935, regarding the above-named patient, who is receiving assistance from our organization. A visit was made to the S home on January 22, 1935. At that time Mr. S was in bed, and he stated that he had followed your recommendations in regard to complete bed rest and has remained quiet since he has returned home.

The S family consists of Mr. S, 46 years old, Mrs. S, 43 years old, a married son, Max, and his wife, and a son Bertram, who is 17 years old. The family occupies a five-room, steam-heated flat on the first floor of a modern building. The home is very well furnished. Mr. and Mrs. S occupy a small bedroom in the rear of the home. The room has one window and contains a bed, dresser, a bureau, and a chair. Mrs. S is a good housekeeper, and the home is very clean.

There appears to be complete harmony in the home, and Mrs. S is very much concerned over Mr. S's health and stated that she is doing the best she can to care for him. However, the family stated that they are having a very difficult time following the diet recommendations on their present budget allowance which consists of a No. 3 B ration box, $7.32, 30 quarts of milk per month, and a grocery order of $11.49. This budget is for three people, as the son Max and his wife are not included in our budget. Max is employed part time and is earning enough to cover his own expenses. We are, therefore, interested in knowing if a special allowance for Mr. S's diet is recommended.

Hoping this information will be of assistance to you in working with Mr. S.

Sincerely yours,
Precinct Supervisor

Another letter shows the subordination of past history to a sharpening of focus on present situation and treatment. Selected history, such as that of employment, is, however, furnished because of the type of agency involved.

Mr. John Doe, Director
Public Welfare Agency
      Re: (Identifying data given here)
My dear . . .

The C family were first known to us on 3-15-33, when Mrs. C applied for financial assistance. At that time Mr. C had been out of work eight or nine months, and Mrs. C, five or six months. Relief has been given on a weekly basis since that time. Mr. C has had only two days' work during a year's contact with the family. Mrs. C has been doing part-time domestic work off and on. Relief has been varied each week, according to the C's income, so that their minimum budget of $12 ($5.25 rent, $5.45 food, $1.20 carfare) has been covered. Clothing in kind has also been given when the C's have expressed a need for it. Total relief during this period has been $451.65.

Mr. C is now receiving treatments regularly at City Hospital Skin Clinic. He started these treatments at Mercy Hospital and was transferred to City Hospital in 8-33. His clinic card is No. 23714D. Mrs. C was also attending Mercy Hospital Clinic but was not admitted at City Hospital Clinic at the time of transfer. We have recently obtained her admittance there and hope that she will soon attend clinic, although she is not anxious to go.

Apparently most of the financial responsibility for the family has been shouldered by Mrs. C for some time, and she has expressed resentment over Mr. C's inactivity. She has often said that if he were working, things would be all right. Mr. C said that he is anxious to work but has been unable to find employment. He feels that his relationship with a private organization has kept him from getting a city job. He has been employed as a porter in the past. Mrs. C has done part-time domestic work. Among her more recent employers are:[1]

.   .   .

[1] Identifying data omitted.

These references have been verified and found satisfactory.

The marital situation seems to be aggravated at times by Iris's presence in the home. Since Iris is not Mr. C's child, Mrs. C often says that he has no right to discipline her. Mr. C says that he is as interested in Iris as if she were his own. Our interviews with Iris have implied that she is not fond of Mr. C. Mrs. C has told us that Iris will do nothing Mr. C tells her, and Mr. C says that Iris is completely disobedient and will not even obey her mother. Mrs. C seems to be particularly interested in keeping Iris neat and clean.

Efforts have been made by us to help the C's towards a better understanding of themselves and their situation. It would seem that the C's do not feel free to discuss matters while they are dependent upon our agency for relief. Recreational facilities for Iris have been discussed, and Iris has joined the Girl Scouts and the YWCA. She is going away to camp for two weeks from June 26 to July 11.

We would like to refer this family to you for full maintenance or possibly for coöperative care. Will you let us know when it would be convenient to have a conference?

Yours very sincerely,

District Secretary

What should be done if it is desirable to send a full transcript of the history? This is resorted to sometimes as a substitute for transferring the case itself, or sometimes as an aid to diagnosis. When Agency B is acting as a consultant, it is still customary to submit a fairly complete history if referring clients for consultant service. Here it is wise to block and arrange the history material, or if the original history is already blocked and arranged, in some cases it is practical to have carbon copies made of the whole work-up which may be sent with a letter of transmittal. Complete case abstracts are rarely exchanged between agencies of the same function. If it is necessary to send such an abstract at all, it is frequently possible to transfer the entire history itself. Such transfers of records have been made during the emergency relief expansion between private and public agencies or frequently between family and child placing agencies, indicating the inherently shared function of such agencies, or between two family agencies. It is the untrained worker who writes to ask for a "complete record of your contact with this family." It is impossible to send such a report without knowing the focus of interest of the inquiring agency.

Outlines for social history are sometimes imposed by the consulting clinic. This practice has inherent difficulties, which it is not here the place to discuss. Some psychiatrists and many judges prefer to have social workers submit studies without any interpretation whatsoever, and as a matter of fact many social workers accede to this. That the person making the study is really the one to interpret it can hardly be disputed. The doctor or judge has his own methods of examination and interpretation of findings, but if study is shared, the interpretation should be shared. If a diagnostic staff conference is not held, it seems more reasonable for each participant to make his own interpretation of that part of the study which he himself does, or the "head" of the staff may take the responsibility for interpreting all findings. In general, the social worker, within the limits of his training and the professional courtesies, should seek to include some interpretation of the material clearly within his own area.

In requesting an out-of-town agency to undertake a difficult interview more circumstantial data are required than in cases in which the client himself is seen by both agencies. The more delicate the mission, the more detail the correspondent will probably need. A clear picture not only of the present problem and proposed treatment but of some of the past events and atti-

tudes, as well as the immediate situation, will be of great
help. In delicate missions, however, one should remember, especially if one's correspondent is not a professional person but a village postmaster, that the letter
may be read aloud to relatives or a former employer.
The word "Confidential" in red written across the top
of the letter does not necessarily insure protection, and
the letter itself must have such dignity, simplicity, and
restraint as to give the least possible cause for offense.
Technical language, dubious at best, should be rigidly
excluded from such correspondence, and the human
interest value included.[2]

In correspondence between agencies conducting a
large amount of shared routine "business" the steering
blank has proved useful. Public welfare departments
communicating with public schools, or family or medical agencies exchanging current information, find the
blank adequate for simple factual reports. The content
of the blank is that of a letter, only more stereotyped,
that is, identifying data, reason for referring, problem
and treatment entered upon by Agency A, a few relevant findings, and a clear request, either general or
specific, of Agency B, make an appropriate communication. If the case is difficult, subtle, or unusual, the
blank will not suffice, and a letter should be substituted.

What then makes for a good inter-agency letter? The
habit of not writing until the case is reasonably well
understood; the reason for writing made clear, which
is usually implicit in a statement of the immediate
treatment situation as faced by Agency A; history
selected so that it bears on the problem under discus-

[2] Cf. the letter to the overseer of the poor in chap. vii.

sion and is subordinated to it; and a frank request for information or assistance, specific if the agency serves a specific function only, more general if the agency written to has a professional rather than a specific service relationship to cases. That is to say, we do not write to doctors and ask them to take Wassermanns, or to family agencies to pay the rent, or to children's agencies to place a child.

It is hardly necessary to mention that all letters should give the exact name and title of the addressee and proper identification of the case. For family agencies the mode of identification is usually the one stereotyped in social service exchange clearings (that is, names and ages of all members of the immediate family), but in writing to agencies like hospitals or courts which may keep a patient index instead of a family index, it is as well to give the patient's name first and underline that. In addition, one should add such administrative identification as may be known, namely, clinic number, ward, court number, which will help in record searching.

VI

THE RECORDING OF PROCESS

CASE work in the last few years has come more and more to focus on problems of relationship, the degree of success with which people handle ordinary life experience, and the satisfactions or dissatisfactions ensuing. In so far as one thinks of people's needs in material or commodity terms, and in so far as case work shapes itself to give units of food, shelter, education, music lessons, convalescent care, and in so far as practical service is uppermost, case recording is likely to be a simple, direct, and easily abbreviated account of what is done. But in so far as case work concerns itself with the rhythms of life expressed in human relationships, we at once are in an area philosophically and technically elusive. Sometimes the case record attempts to reproduce the movement within a single interview between worker and client. Sometimes the record attempts to show interchange in group process, such as a family conversation. Sometimes the content is merely the verbal exchange plus any very marked behavior; sometimes gesture, bodily postures, and tensions are fully noted. Sometimes the worker's impressions, as well as words and actions, are given. There is no way of determining whether the attempt to reproduce behavior and conversation is reasonably accurate. Some workers have far better trained memories and far better control of their emotional biases than others. Some workers make notes while interviewing; others do not.[1] Even though an interview be dictated verbatim immediately after its termination much will escape both notes and recollection. Whether this method gives us more or less accurate material than when it is analyzed and arranged, one cannot say. One can only say that the reproduction is undertaken in the hope of indicating the manner in which one person appears to relate himself to another person during the therapeutic experience.

Workers have always debated the question as to how much of mechanics or procedure belongs in records. Clearly it is a waste of time to write "Telephoned Grand Central Station and ascertained that train left at 3:15, called at home, waited while mother dressed Johnny and took him in a bus to the station." If during these arrangements either Johnny's or his mother's behavior or conversation was significant, a descriptive entry might be valuable, but the worker's behavior and technique are in this example unimportant. Pioneer social case workers trying to learn a technique of social investigation in the face of much hostile criticism did describe the mechanics of steps taken with more detail than would be useful today, when such procedures are quite well understood, accepted, and obvious. For a teaching record a surgeon may describe an operation carefully, but he does not begin the record with his procedure in washing up with green soap. In case work, as we have said before, the student must be taught not to neglect the obvious, but this does not mean that he should record details of the obvious. The search in all social case work is for the significant,

---

[1] For full transcriptions of two cases, see Taft, Jessie, *The Dynamics of Therapy*, The Macmillan Company. 1933.

and recording should be only of material which we
think has (out of the world of things which one sees
and touches in any social situation) at least potential
significance in treatment. The careful writer tends thus
to delete purely routine details, appointments, the activities in steering and executive treatment, and to give
results alone whenever the steps involved in those
results would be understood by another professional
worker. The best rule about recording mechanics or
procedure is to report only what is unusual. We would
not say: "Called and found Mrs. Smith at home" or
"Called and did not find Mrs. Smith at home"; but we
would say "Called for the third consecutive day and
was unable to find Mrs. Smith, although she has said
that she had no work at all."

In the first two decades of the century when the
workers concerned themselves chiefly with the study
and analysis of facts and events objectively considered,
the records were episodic and static like photographs.
In the third decade, under psychiatric and then psy-
choanalytical influences, behavior was studied, first
descriptively and then more and more for its meaning
to the client. Then, as the assumption was made that
only the client could give the meaning for him, the
interest turned from the history of behavior to con-
versational behavior or the interview. "History," Miss
Robinson says, "will take its place in the relationship
. . . as one of the client's reactions. It will come into
the record at whatever time and place the client needs
to make use of it . . ."[2] The attempt "to see things in
their own order and conviction," as Spinoza phrased it,

<hr>

[2] Robinson, Virginia, *A Changing Psychology in Social Case Work,* p.
143, University of North Carolina Press, 1930.

was precipitated into case work largely through interpretation of the treatment relationship. Recording at once reflected this preoccupation, and emotional material as revealed by the client's demands, fears, and aggression was lifted into the foreground of the picture.

The recording of process is usually confined to the process and movement within the interview and not used within a series of events or episodes which instead are abbreviated or summarized in most records. The case worker may reproduce an interview in a two-dimensional effect of what I did and he did, what I said and he said, as in the following two examples:

DIRECT TREATMENT[3]

Process of interview shown

But she does not want us to talk with George about moving. We asked whether he did not want to move. She replied that he does not; he thinks she is better off with her mother. Then she added, "I keep the terrible things that go on from him so he really does not understand how bad it is. Then when I do tell him he tells me to go upstairs and not listen to my mother or to forget about what she says, that I am taking things too seriously." We said, "Maybe you are." She replied that she could not help it. She knows how her mother feels about her so she can see through the remarks she makes. Nobody else knows just how things are, not even George. She does not want him to know or he would not go on living there. We asked whether that was not what she had just said she wanted, that if she wanted to move and he wanted to move, everything would work out nicely. She simply replied, as though dismissing the subject, that she supposed she might as well forget it and stay there. We remarked that we thought

[3] The term "relationship treatment," used in the first edition was never wholly satisfactory to the writer, but the practices and concepts in the field do not as yet supply an adequate phrase. The terms "direct treatment" and "therapy" are used by some case workers. Without going into an analysis of the concepts behind these terms we may simply say that the illustrations following in this chapter are to show how interviews may be recorded, not how treatment may be given.

she probably never had any intention of moving and that there must be some reason why, in the face of so many objections, she still wanted to stay at home. She laughed nervously, saying that she supposed she would miss her mother and father even though her mother was a devil. We said, "What about your father, is he a devil too?" Her reply was that he was all right.

In the next illustration the worker's part, although not so active, is none the less clear.

DIRECT TREATMENT
Process of interview shown

Mr. W sat looking at this card, tapping it against his finger, and said, "I wonder where this is all going to get me. Every place you go you have to wait so long, and they ask you so many questions. Do you think I like to come to a place like this? This was not my idea, it was my wife's. I wouldn't come here. What is the good of all these questions and the red tape you have to go through? Don't they believe you? Do you think I would come here and lie for a couple of dollars? Do you think I would make myself go through this if I had any money?" Mr. W stopped suddenly and leaned toward worker, looking directly at her. "Where do you think I'll get by being square?" He repeated, "Where do you think it will get me? You ought to be able to tell me that. You have lots of fellows coming in here to talk to you. What do you answer people if they ask you that?" Worker said that she did not feel there was a general answer you could give to everyone as to where they would get by being square. It depended so much on the person's own feeling and how much they thought it would mean to them to be on the square. Mr. W sat quietly. "I suppose you're right, everybody's not the same. They don't feel the same way about it. Well, I know this about me, it wouldn't be worth it to me to risk ten years in jail for a few hundred dollars, but if I were in on a big job that would bring me plenty of money, I might take a chance." Mr. W continued, saying that he had never got into any trouble yet, but that sometimes he did think about it. "I get sick and disgusted when I can't find a job. I think of all my clothes in the pawn shop." Mr. W told worker that he had gone to several of his friends and tried to borrow money so that his wife would not have to come here and ask for help, but none of them could give him anything. Several of these he had loaned money to many times. "Sometimes I think I'm a fool not to chuck the whole thing and get out. I could have done it, but I stayed." Mr. W sat looking down at his hat, and worker asked if he knew why he had stayed. "I don't know. I figured that I might be able to find something. My wife would be in a pretty tight place if I did go away. I am going to try and stick it out now. My wife has some different ideas from me, but I let her go her own way. I never stand in the way of anything she wants to do." Worker asked Mr. W what he meant by different ideas that his wife had from him. "She likes things different from me." Mr. W explained that she wanted to study and get herself a good job. "That's all right if she wants to. I think she has a right to her way of thinking the same as I have to mine. I wouldn't mind learning a little myself, but I'd be satisfied with things as they are if I only had a job and had enough to eat, and if we could go out and have a good time once in a while." Mr. W said that he had been used to going to the Dixie Club and Spear's Cabaret and now he couldn't go anywhere.

The following illustration, like the first, clearly shows the worker's role. Obviously we are not debating about whether, when, and how to interpret but are showing interviews in which what is said is recorded.

DIRECT TREATMENT
Process of interview shown

We asked if there were any particular reason why he felt he couldn't ask us again, whereupon he said that he really was sort of mad the last time he was here. He just couldn't understand us, to refuse a man a pair of shoes when he needed them so badly. Why if Mr. W had anything at all he couldn't refuse a man a pair of shoes when his feet were hanging out that way. He just couldn't understand it. As he walked up the Avenue from the office he kept saying to himself, "Why did she refuse me?" We wondered if he had thought of any answer and he said he couldn't for the life of him think of any reason. He needed them so badly. Was he rude or something like that? He couldn't have been rude. He's not that kind. Gee, even the children could tell how mad he was. He hadn't meant to tell us, but he just couldn't figure it out. Not that it made any difference to us refusing him. It was all in a day's work to us. We commented that in a way he felt that we had refused him because we didn't like him. He said that he couldn't imagine that that was it. Why, he felt sure that we liked him. Why wouldn't we? Why, there wasn't anything wrong in that, was there? He liked us and we liked him. He just couldn't understand. He looked at us confidentially and said, "Why did you do it? Was it the budget?" Then he went on to say that he thought perhaps we didn't have any more money that month. We commented that we had hurt him by refusing him shoes and he said, "Honest, you did." We said that was as though by not giving him what he asked for we were telling him that we didn't like him. He said it was funny but it sort of seemed that way. He thought we wanted to help a person. Why he'd give the shirt off his back to anybody who needed anything as badly as he needed those shoes. He just couldn't understand it. He liked us—he thought we were a good sort and then what a surprise it was to him to see his feet sticking through. We remembered the hole, didn't we? We nodded and he spoke about the pain he had had when he walked. Why his feet ached. He pointed to his feet and said, "You see, I got a pair now." He got them the very next pay day after he had been in. He just took the money and bought them. They cost $3.30. "Gee, I was mad at you." We commented that he had thought that we liked him enough to give him what he asked for and that we had let him down and didn't want to help him any more. When we didn't give him the shoes, it was as though we were telling him that we didn't like him and he would wonder about all the reasons for this. He said that he didn't think for a moment that it made any difference to us, refusing a pair of shoes or not. We said that was the thing that hurt most of all, wasn't it? He said he guessed it was, and he just couldn't figure it out.

We said that it was hard to think that we were a person who saw quite a lot of people and that we didn't see him just as a friend. He said he supposed that was true.

Another illustration shows more of a dialogue arrangement but similar influence:

DIRECT TREATMENT[4]

Process of interview shown

Mother then exclaimed: "But I am not content. That is why I came here today. My sister-in-law is coming to visit and I am going to leave home. I am going to leave my husband."

Worker: "What does your husband feel about this sister?" *Mother wept, saying:* "She is his favorite and he is hers. He is the oldest—this sister next. He dislikes his two younger sisters, but I like them."

Worker: "What do you dislike most about her visit?" *Mother:* "I'm afraid of what she will say about me to my husband." *Worker:* "Have you felt this way before?" Mother then talked of her unhappiness in the home of the relatives following her marriage. She did not understand their language, but she felt their dislike. She learned the language quickly to find out what they were saying to her husband against her.

Worker: "I understand how you must have felt. What had you hoped to find in marriage?" Mother said she had built no air castles even though her husband had promised to make her rich. Her mother had warned her against expecting the impossible. She had, however, been sorry to leave her mother and sister and had looked forward to finding a substitute for them in her husband's relatives. She cried again as she told of the "meanness" of these relatives and of her wish to return to her home when she realized they hated her.

Worker: "Why is it hard for you to accept hate? What has been your experience with it?" *Mother:* "I never knew what it was in my childhood. I was the favorite. I was never nervous. My sister was, and we quarreled often. She was two years younger. She got more attention from my father, because she was sick. He gave her oranges, but I was his favorite, because I was smart. I felt more secure with my mother. My father did not like my boy friends. I don't remember my brothers; they were much younger." When asked where this sister is now

[4] Since the first edition of this book, this material, in substantially the same form, has appeared in *Psychiatric Social Service in a Children's Hospital,* by Ruth M. Gartland, The University of Chicago Press, 1937.

living, mother says she is married, has a girl patient's age, is now pregnant, and lives with her parents.

To help mother face her hostile feelings and work through her guilt for them, worker said, "You say you quarreled with your sister?" *Mother:* "Yes, I was glad when I could tell my mother about some mischief she had been doing. Sister let things out; I kept them in." *Worker:* "You were the good child." Mother nodded (a long pause) then she exclaimed, "Why that's what I've been all my life. You asked me once if I liked people, wanted more recreation, more social life, and I said I did not. After I returned home I thought over what you had asked and realized that I do like people, but my husband does not. I have been the good child and agreed with his ideas. Perhaps it makes me nervous to keep things in." She fears another nervous breakdown if she has to endure the visit of her husband's sister as she did that of her mother-in-law, silently. When asked if there was anything different in this situation she replied, "Yes, I won't have to keep things in—I can talk to you."

Mother then talked about her husband. When they were first married, he took her part. Now he blames her for her antagonism to his relatives. He is irritable with her. He is "always right" and "won't listen" when mother says he is wrong. He does not like to have her meet other men or to go out with friends. He won't share recreation with her, feeling it is a waste of time. Mother said, "I want help in understanding him."

Worker: "With whom can we afford to be irritable?" *Mother* (after a pause) : "With those who will go on caring anyway?" Worker agreed that acquaintances would not put up with irritability, and therefore we get rid of our anxieties with those who will understand and keep on caring. *Mother:* "Then perhaps he is anxious about something else when he is cross with me." *Worker:* "Yes, and most secure with you. His need of you is shown by his wish to keep you from friends who might take you from him; by his wish to have you think him right." *Mother:* "I suppose when I tell him he's wrong, it makes him think I don't love him."

In the moving picture we are shown behavior or action in a perfectly controlled reproduction which may or may not be aided by titles. In the drama, "asides" have always been used to interpret the action, and this device is a favorite with Eugene O'Neill. The novelist may assume complete insight into the feelings and thought processes of his characters. In the case record the remarks of the client and the stimulus remarks of the worker are commonly shown, and with these may be included parenthetical diagnostic impressions or comments.

Another illustration, showing the handling of a desertion case, brings out clearly some of the worker-client interaction.

DIRECT TREATMENT

Process of interview shown

Mrs. B in Office. She starts the interview by saying that George is all right now. She then makes a few comments and asks some questions about his working papers. Worker feels that these are an attempt to make conversation. She then pauses a moment and says that she had heard nothing from Mr. B. Worker asks if she felt just the same. She says that she does. She finds that she is still thinking. Worker asks if she is still going over the past in the same way. She says that she is more or less. She does not know; she cannot seem to get it out of her mind. She does not know whether he will come back or not. She cannot think about the future. She has tried, but she just doesn't know what to think. She would rather wait a couple of months and see whether she will hear from Mr. B again. If she does not hear from him, then she will be thinking about the future. Worker asks if she thinks chiefly about whether she will go back to Mr. B or not. She nods. If he will only come back here, that will settle everything, but she does not know what she would do if she got a letter from him from Pittsburgh. Should she go back again? If she should get a letter from Mr. B, she would come right in and ask worker's advice. She asks if worker would give her advice. Worker says perhaps we could help Mrs. B to make up her own mind what she would like to do. She continues by saying that she does not want to deprive the boys of a father. She pauses and says, "You see, that is what happened to me." Her mother married when she was very young. "You see," she explains, "it is the same thing as with my husband. He listened to his own family instead of considering his wife and children." Mrs. B feels that she has always been deprived of a father's love. He died not long after that. After his death they all went to live with one of Mrs. B's uncles. He was very good to them, but she has never felt that it was the same as having a father. Her mother could not forgive her father. She has not wanted to make the same mistake. That is why she has always gone back and forgiven her husband. Perhaps she has made the opposite mistake.

. . .

As she does not go on, worker says that last week Mrs. B made a remark that worker got to thinking about, and she wondered what Mrs. B meant. Worker repeats Mrs. B's remark about it being her fault, that she made a mistake again in her decision. Mrs. B explains that if the time comes to decide, she wants advice so she will not make a mistake again. She does not want advice now; she wants to go on thinking things through. If she hears from Mr. B, then she wants to feel that she can come in and ask worker. Now she wants just to try and figure it out. She keeps on thinking about things. (She speaks slowly with considerable emotion in her voice.) Her remarks are often abrupt. She says that there is really no one she trusts. She felt she could talk to former visitor, and now she feels she can talk to visitor. She thinks that they can help her. Her sister and her mother are prejudiced; she cannot go to them. When the time comes, she will tell worker what she thinks, and worker can tell her whether she is right or wrong. Worker remarks that perhaps it is not a question of right or wrong. Mrs. B asks, "You don't think so?" She feels that the boys need their father. They are fond of him; they ask for him a great deal. He was always good to them. She does not know whether it is a sense of duty that makes her want to go back.

. . .

Without pausing for comment she goes on, saying that her brother thinks she loves Mr. B too much. She does not know just what it is. She thinks that she has fairly accurate premoni-

tions about things. She has had them before. Not only about
the good things, but about the bad things; and now she feels
that she is going to hear from Mr. W and that there will be
a job for Mr. B. She pauses a moment or two and smiles; of
course, that is what she wants. They say that sometimes we
want things one way, but God doesn't quite figure things
that way. She wants God to be on her side this time. Worker
asks if she feels that everything will be solved if Mr. B gets
a job here. Mrs. B smiles; she does not quite think that, she
thinks it is the most important thing. She speaks of the incidents that occurred in the past and of the way she tried to
get Mr. B to come back; then he could blame her. If he comes
back this time, it will be because things are not so good in
Pittsburgh and because he wants to come home. She feels
that before his sister and mother were always pulling and in-
fluencing him this way and that. Of course she realizes that
he is weak. She would not be influenced that way. If her
family wanted her to go somewhere without him, she could
not do it, because she would not feel right; but he is not like
that. He could leave her and go to his family. He has always
been able to do that. But she thinks that maybe he can learn
by experience, and anyhow his sister is dead now; his mother
is not well—may not live long. She cannot do as much for
him, and after all he needs to have things done for him. She
does not mind doing them. She can do his washing along with
hers. She appeals to worker. Does not worker think that perhaps he will have learned by experience this time? Worker
replies that perhaps a great many of the influences have been
on the outside, but does not Mrs. B think that also, as far
as Mr. B is concerned, a great many of the pulls come from
inside himself? Perhaps they will still be there. He does, of
course, partly want to be with her and the children. Mrs. B
says that that is so. The thing is that he wants to please everybody.

.   .   .

Mrs. B goes on as if thinking aloud in a rather jumbled
fashion. She brings up the question of the whole situation
being his mother's responsibility—her coming here in the first
place—admitting that it was partly her own doing because
she wanted to come. She speaks of a remark of her mother's
that she will be a saint, and denies that. But she thinks she

is going to win. She thinks things are going to come her way. Does not worker think so? Worker says she thinks that that is what Mrs. B wants very badly to happen.

Mrs. B does not know what she will do if Mr. B does not come back. She thinks she should get some other interest so that she will not be thinking of this all the time. She wonders if Mr. B thinks about her and the children as much as she thinks about him. Does worker think he does? Worker says that she does not know; Mrs. B knows him better than she does. Mrs. B asks if worker would like to know what Mr. B said about her when he came in? Worker asks, what? Mrs. B replies that he thought worker was hard-hearted, more hard-hearted than former worker. Worker replies, "perhaps you think so too." Mrs. B says no. She speaks of thinking worker was partly right in not sympathizing too much with Mr. B. That is the trouble with him—he wants too much sympathy. He plays for that. It is better in a way not to have it. Worker is young, much younger than Mrs. B. Yet Mrs. B feels she understands. Mrs. B does not believe if she were in worker's place she could handle someone so well. She indicates that she would be more identified, more sympathetic. Worker would not be able to tell her to be hard-hearted too. Worker remarks that she is not telling Mrs. B to be hard-hearted, but she is telling Mrs. B that Mrs. B thinks she is hard-hearted. Mrs. B says no, she thought so at first; she does not really think so any more.

The time cost both for reading and recording in this manner is high; it is hard for any but the most highly-trained interviewer to catch significant associations; and, fundamentally, one wonders whether science or art can reproduce so subtle a matter as a treatment relationship. It is reported that Nijinsky was fascinated by the problem of trying to reproduce and score dance rhythms as music is scored, but found the task baffling. Many current records trying to show relationship through process—that is, interviewing process—are cumbersome, banal, and extravagant, if not actually absurd. Yet for study, self-supervisory, and teaching purposes it is interesting to have this material available as accurately and completely as the limitation of recall and transcription will permit. Later, growing skill may permit a more selective handling.

Since the recording of relationship treatment is being so much experimented with, we should perhaps give another example. One cannot do justice to complicated case material through these illustrations removed from the context, but the discriminating reader will see a conscious direction and control in the interviews cited which are quite different from the untrained worker's attempt to reproduce what remains a conversation, not an interview.

DIRECT TREATMENT

Process of interview shown

Eleanor paused then said, "It was different when my sisters and brother were at home. My father and mother were younger then, and they did not have to worry so much." Worker said, "This has seemed unfair to you?" Eleanor said almost explosively that it had seemed very unfair. She had felt all alone "holding up everything." Her mother could not decide anything and always was asking her what she thought. "You know she is that way." Then her father had to get sick and couldn't plan. "It just seemed as if someone had to do something, and there was only me. There was nothing I could do, and I felt as if I had to, but couldn't." She paused. "It is very hard to describe. The others never had a time like this." Worker said, "Your sisters and brother?" And Eleanor nodded.

"Oh, my father understands me some, but there are things even he cannot understand, and (scornfully) my mother does not understand me at all. You know, she couldn't." Slight pause. "Oh, it seems awful to talk this way. I suppose you think I am terribly selfish." Worker said, "You have felt selfish?" Eleanor nodded. She had felt that she should not think it mean that everything fell on her, yet she couldn't help it. It just came to her mind sometimes, and she pushed it back. She looked at worker directly and said, "You know, I think that's what makes me nervous."

After a slight pause she said, "You know, at camp the most wonderful thing happened. I thought I was going to have a spell, and I said to myself that I mustn't have a spell; and you know, I got all drawn up inside, but I never did have a real spell." Worker wondered why she felt this was so. Eleanor said, "I think I had too many other things to think about. There were always things I wanted to do. There were games and plans we were making, and I think I just didn't have time to think of it; but I was so happy when I found I could control the spells and that I didn't have to have them, and I thought I didn't need to have them any more. I had worried before going to camp. I thought 'suppose I have a spell and there is no one there to help me!' I wanted to go to camp so much, so I just thought, 'well, I won't have them,' and then when I didn't, it was wonderful." She paused. "You know, I don't know whether I ought to go to my aunt and uncle or not. I have thought so much about it. What do you think?" Worker wondered if Eleanor would be satisfied with anyone's decision but her own. She smiled and said maybe she wouldn't.

"I think, maybe, like I told you before, I feel as if, if I go away from all this I would drop everything behind me." Worker said, "Everything?" Eleanor nodded and said more slowly, "Everything being on my shoulders and doing (in a low voice) that thing I don't like—as if I could leave it all behind and do something different." Worker wondered if she had felt that she might have any difficulties on this trip. She smiled and said, "I know what you mean."

After a pause and half laughing she said she guessed the newness had worn off. She does not feel she is getting along so well. Perhaps she had looked forward too much. Worker said "You are discouraged?" She nodded slowly. They have not heard from South Africa yet. She finally wrote her aunt but is wondering what she will answer. Then the newness of the house has worn off. It was exciting when they first went there, but now there is nothing new about it to think about. She paused, then said abruptly, "It is terrible to be like that!" Worker said, "To be like that?"; and she said "to always need something new and exciting to keep you going all right." She looked at worker and said "Isn't it a bad thing to be?" Worker wondered if there were particular reasons why she felt it was. She said that it kept her unhappy so much of the time. She would plan ahead and be excited and then get disappointed. She thought she should be able to control it. She repeated as she has before, "I'm so changeable. First I like a thing, and then I don't. One day I feel like doing something, and another day just the opposite." Worker asked if she was thinking of anything in particular. She said that one day she would feel very affectionate; the next she would not want to have anyone come near her. Rather quickly she said, with vehemence, that the one thing she could not stand for was to have a friend go back on her. If anyone did her a bad turn, she could never feel the same toward that person again. If someone failed her just once, things could never be the same. She did not know why this was, but supposed it was just her nature. Worker queried, "You felt that way because of the broken appointments here?" She replied coldly but politely that she understood that worker had been called away on business. Worker said, "You thought I might have let you know ahead?" Eleanor nodded, and worker said that since she felt this way and since there had been no time to let her know about the change in appointments, worker felt that Eleanor should know the reason.

After a little flushing she said, "I suppose it sounds terrible to say you mind things about your own mother, but I don't mean it that way. She can't help it—it's just the ways she has." Worker wondered what she minded. She said "Oh, she doesn't understand things—she can't talk like my father, and she, you know, can take anything. She doesn't mind things that are not quite nice. I don't think she knows them. She can't advise me as my father can." After a slight pause she said rather abruptly, "My father and mother never kiss. I don't think I have ever seen them kiss." She smiled. "Forty years of marriage—that sounds like a lot, doesn't it?" Growing more sober she said that neither of her parents likes touching and showing affection. She often teases her father by touching him or patting him, coming up behind him and putting her arms around him. "He doesn't like it a bit." Thoughtfully she said that perhaps her parents were more affectionate when they first got married. She is glad that they were not so young when she was born. She thinks it would be terrible to have young parents. "You know they would be all for pleasure and what fun they could have themselves, and a child would feel out of it." She has always been thankful for this, although she has heard people say it is better for parents to be young. She does not know whether she could have stood it to have them so interested in each other and herself left out. Then she repeated, "It sounds terrible," but her feeling for her father is because they have so much in common.

She wondered if worker thought it was right to divorce. Supposing the man fell in love with someone else, and she with him. Did he have a right to divorce his wife? Worker wondered how she felt about it, and she said she thought that if there were no children he had a right. If there were children, they should stay together for the sake of the children. Did worker feel that this was so? Worker wondered if she were the child, how she would feel about it. She said "That's right. I might be." Then more slowly she said that she would not want her father and mother to stay together because of her, if they were unhappy. She did not think it would be so pleasant. It would be terrible, though, because she would not know which one to choose, if she had to choose between. She would, of course, choose her father, but she did not think she could hurt her mother's feelings by choosing him.

Some writers advise that application interviews be in part at least reproduced, since through the client's own story in his own words his sense of problem is brought out more clearly. Thereafter they would restrict verbatim recording to interviews or series of interviews or selections from interviews in which therapeutic movement seems involved. Case workers are trying to discriminate between material which inherently need not be reproduced in full, because it is obvious or manageable in other ways, and material which seems to call for notations as intricate as Nijinsky's choreography.

Some writers are now trying to record through a

sort of "streamline" picture. The arrangement is still chronological and natural, but the quoted material or cited behavior is highly selective. Nevertheless, the following will illustrate the attempt to substitute selected incidents and remarks for full verbatim process. It is not unlike the periodic summary given in an earlier chapter. The difference, if any, lies in the fact that the attempt at condensation, under the process influence, is of behavior and interviewing, and not so much of events, and services. How possible it is to "streamline" with a free use of asterisks a series of treatment interviews, it is too soon to say. Verbatim recording is unreliable without the use of extensive notes taken in the presence of client, which is usually not practicable, or else immediately afterward, a method which, with training, can be made serviceable although not scientific.

PERIODIC SUMMARY[5]

Cyril has been seen once every week since his placement in the foster home 11/25/31. During this time his attitude toward his mother has not changed. He becomes upset whenever her name is mentioned, shivers, pales, and is very tense. Because of this an attempt is made to avoid any mention of Mrs. X in Cyril's presence. He is constantly assured that under no circumstances will he be forced to return to her, but he is allowed to express his fears verbally in order to rid himself of some of the emotional tension. In order to divert his attention to other things, temporary membership at the Center was arranged 1/12/32. However, the boy reported that he

[5] In place of four separate entries. For the second edition of this book the writer has hesitated especially about the inclusion of the first of the three periodic summaries, because the case work indicated raises so many questions. The reasons for deciding to include it were the same reasons which determined other selections, namely, that the attempt to record the substance of interviews is valid and that there is no doubt but that better understanding of case work would change the content, even though these and other shortening devices were used.

would not enjoy the Center or the swimming because "I'm always thinking about what she will do if she wins the trial." On 1/15/32 he appeared to be extremely upset and voiced some new fears. As soon as he was alone with worker he blurted out, "I called her on the phone to ask how she was. She yelled into the receiver since when was I interested how she was and why didn't I come to see her. Then I let Mrs. T speak to her. I was too afraid. I wouldn't go to see her. You know what she would do to me. She would take me into the garage and cut me up into little pieces. You don't know my mother." Worker tried to reassure him that people do not kill other people so easily and that his mother was just as afraid of the law as any other person. "Oh, you don't know my mother. She could do anything when she's mad. When she makes a face at me, I know it's murder. She always said she would rather kill me than have my father get custody of me." Cyril was reminded that his mother had quarreled with his father and been separated from him for a long time and had never done him any violence, why then need he worry now? "Oh, she's getting even with him through me. I tell you, if she wins the trial, as soon as we get to the station, I'll run away. I must. Don't be angry if I do. I just got to, 'cause it will mean murder, especially after all the bad things I'll say about her in court. Gee, I'm worried. Even if my father wins the case, I'm worried. I'll want a private detective to guard me and my father, because she'll kill us both. I know it." Cyril mentioned the fact that the assistant principal had also tried to encourage him not to worry, that she would do everything she could to influence the judge to award the father custody of him. "But it's no use. I can't help worrying." When worker tried to change the subject to his health, Cyril said, "Yes, I feel better this week, last week I was pretty sick. Mrs. T made me take castor oil. I didn't want to take it because I wanted to get sicker and die. If I die, then I won't have to worry any more." Again worker tried to assure him that the agency was doing everything that it could, and gradually the conversation shifted to the foster home. "They're wonderful to me, and since Sarah spoke to you she treats me great. Like a brother. Frank, too; he took me to the show with him." The remainder of the hour was spent discussing the show he had seen. In subsequent interviews in the office,

Cyril reiterated these same fears about his mother. He was grateful for everything that the school and the agency were trying to do for him, but he was still afraid. He was impatient for the trial to be over. On 2/10/32 worker discussed the situation with the assistant principal. She has taken a fancy to Cyril and is willing to do anything to help him. His reactions to his mother in the school are the same as those in the office. Cyril has explained the whole situation to the assistant principal, and she, who has seen Mrs. X, is sympathetic to him. He is constantly voicing his fear of his mother. He once remarked to the assistant principal that if he were a girl he was sure his mother would sell him into white slavery. When the assistant principal saw that none of her assurances seemed to help the boy, she frankly told him that if he had to die, he would, and that none of his worrying would do him any good, and that he had better make the most of his life in the meantime. Cyril had told worker of this incident with the remark, "I guess she's right. But I wish the trial was over." The trial according to Mr. X is scheduled for the middle of February. A definite date has not been set.

PERIODIC SUMMARY

From unrecorded notes[6]

In interview of 1-14, Anna expressed her regret that Ethel had not won in the memory contest. When asked whether she really cared that Ethel had not won, she said that she had wanted Ethel to win just to show those 7A-rapid advance kids a thing or two. She seemed to identify with Ethel at this point in her striving to be smarter than her own rapid advance class. On 1-18, she discussed the fact that she was no longer very friendly with Ethel though she continued to see her. She laughed as she said that they got along all right but that was probably because they didn't see so much of each other. In both the interviews of 1-14 and 1-18, Anna spoke of how smoothly she and her mother were getting along. Her mother has been very nice to her and Anna in turn has been obedient. She has been willing to take cod liver oil because her mother explained to her that it was a muscle builder. Being stubborn with her father was "the general thing" and in both interviews she spoke of the fact that she not only was like her father who

---

[6] In place of two entries.

couldn't give in, but she couldn't give in to him. Both of them were stubborn with the result that they usually fought.

In both interviews, Anna spoke of "romance," partly in jest and partly in seriousness. She flippantly remarked that it wasn't much use having a sweetheart because he could always pick up another girl. Then you were left heart-broken and perhaps would have to commit suicide, unless you were a "heart-breaker" yourself. She spoke of wanting romance in her life, but the thoughts that she had about it were secret. When I said that I thought we were not to have any secrets here, she spoke of the fact that she had "the hopes of a girl" even though she liked to wear pants and climb. When asked what these hopes were, she said that she liked to wash her doll's clothes and had spent time doing this and sewing last Saturday. With some hesitation, she said that she also wanted a baby though of course she preferred a boy. When asked if there were anything else, she said that this was all but added that she thought I didn't believe that there was nothing else to her secret. I said that if she said so, then I believed her and if at any time she had more secrets, I thought she would tell me. Anna once more mentioned the new boy in her class and said she had not yet had an opportunity to get to know him. She brought out the fact that she never struck girls but did strike the smaller boys. All the small boys had received at least one blow from her. The reason for this was that the smaller boys could protect themselves better than the girls. With this she also tied up the fact that she was still afraid of Gloria.

Anna came a few minutes late for both of these interviews. When she expressed concern over the lateness for the second time, on 1-18, I asked her why she was worried about it. She said she didn't like being late. It was as if she were breaking an appointment. This may be the beginning of a more direct expression of aggression toward me.

PERIODIC SUMMARY[7]

From unrecorded notes

On these three occasions the interviews with Alice were quite productive. Alice kept the appointments fairly promptly and had a good deal to say. She went over some of the material she had previously given us regarding her early ex-

---

[7] In place of three separate entries.

periences and her attitude, past and present, regarding her family. She also added some new material.

Interview on 11/11 was one of the few interviews in which Alice was direct in introducing the discussion of her family's problem. After talking of relief Alice informed the worker that she had had a miserable week at home. She told about this and then went on to discuss some of the things that had happened to her earlier. In the interviews of 11/20 and 11/29, Alice was less direct about introducing a discussion of her problems. However, her desire to do so was clear, and she responded to worker's effort to help lead into this. That Alice does want to talk of her problems is clear. For several reasons Alice and the worker both feel some discomfort at the point where Alice has finished what she wished to say about the practical situation and doesn't know how to get into discussion of the psychological situation. Once this bridge is crossed the tension is relaxed. Worker attempted to handle the matter in the interview of 11/29. At this time Alice was facing her problem with us more clearly than she had before. After talking of the experiences which have made her and her situation such as they are, she said that she was "in a mess." She wished someone could show her a way out. She couldn't see a way herself. Worker said that there were no easy ways out and that no one could find the way except Alice. We asked then if thinking about the things that had happened to her and talking to us about them helped her to see things more clearly. Perhaps in this way she might be able to find a way out. Alice did not answer the question directly. She said in a discouraged tone of voice that she guessed the worker was right. She was the only one who could get herself out of her present situation. She added that it wasn't her fault that she was "in a mess." It was a result of the things that had happened to her. It is the experiences which people have that make them what they are. Worker agreed and said Alice had had many hard experiences.

She then said that she hadn't ever talked about her family affairs before. She had only talked to worker and recently to a friend. (This friend Alice had told us about in the interview of 11/11.) Alice had not seen this friend of hers in a number of years. They had lost track of each other. Several weeks previous the friend had found out where they were living and called on them. From Alice's account, it is apparent that the friend has always been sympathetic with Alice's troubles and identified with her in her hostility toward John. Alice had apparently let out a good deal of her feeling to this friend who had taken her side before Mrs. P and her mother had told John what she thought of him. The friend said that John didn't appreciate what Alice had been doing. If he were left on his own he would realize things.

Alice discussed her work telling us how she enjoyed it. She prefers the sort of work she does to anything else. She never wanted to do stenographic work, for which she had been trained. That isn't interesting. She cried as she said that because of the way she felt about her family, she no longer likes her work. She wants to like it again.

Alice said that they never had much money and that she had had to have her lunches free at school. Also she had obtained shoes from the school when her mother had not had the money for them. Alice told this when discussing her feeling about coming to us for help. She said that John hadn't had to get things free from the school. Alice laughed as she said that she had been so glad when we had asked him to come in last fall. He hadn't seen any reason for doing so, but she was glad he had to do it. It never occurred to him that he should have as much responsibility as she. Alice concluded that she couldn't expect much from him, ever. He had had an excellent job in a sugar can company, and he gave the job up. He had had the same job for four seasons in succession and was earning very good money. He could have gone back for the fifth season, but he didn't. He preferred to come here and study, while she worked for him. There were schools there, too, but he would have been criticized so much there if he had tried to do what he has done here. Here people criticize him, too, but there are not so many people who know them.

In talking of the fact that she had had so few playmates when young, Alice said that even when she was a young child she and John didn't get along. He was always selfish. She also brought out that he is only two years older than she is, not eight as we had thought. Alice told of going out with him once in South America because her mother forced him to take her with him. Naturally, being a boy, he wasn't restricted as she was. Alice's resentment about this was manifest. Alice told of another time when she went some place with John. That was when the talking pictures first came out. John asked her to go to a movie with him. With marked disgust and hatred in her voice, Alice told us how she had had to pay for the tickets. She seemed angry at herself for having accepted his invitation in the first place. She said that he had never done anything nice for her as long as she could remember. She knows that he hates her. She told of John's having told her once that he was the man of the family.

The budget was rediscussed on 11/11. (See budget filed) Alice mentioned that coal was so expensive that they were finding it hard to manage on the money. The food budget was calculated, and it came to $9. Her cousin is giving $4 of this. Other items Alice enumerated were 60¢ for cleaning and household supplies, 60¢ for carfare, and 20¢ for health care. She was able to meet these items at present from her earnings, she said. Therefore we agreed to give $5 (which they were short of) for food. Relief during the period was as follows: 11/11, $6 for food; 11/18, $14.83 expended for a ton of coal; 11/20, $5 for food; 11/29, $5 for food.

Attempts to reproduce group interrelationship are still rare. The following illustration, although containing only slight treatment elements, is in this area. The recording does not differ from that used in the interview, and no new forms appear to be utilized.

GROUP INTERACTION[8]

On the worker's arrival in the home, Mr. and Mrs. C were cordial and gracious. Mr. C, who was sitting at the table toying with a pencil and paper, initiated the interview with the statement that he had been put on work relief and would have his first day's work on Friday. He started to tell more of this when Mrs. C interrupted excitedly to tell of the family's debts, the long overdue rent, the fact that they had had to get "trust" to have the electricity again turned on, the children's graduation, etc. Mrs. C seemed terribly upset and continued so for the greater part of the visit. She leaned across

[8] Other and more interesting experiments in group interaction must be sought in group work records.

the table, stared fixedly, and several times appeared to be on the verge of tears. Occasionally when she did not go on, Mr. C threw out some remark about the inadequacy of the Work Relief pay. For the most part Mr. C looked down at the table and held his head in his hands.

Although Mrs. C was in turn angry and despairing as she spoke, her animosity did not appear to be against the worker. It was noticed that she dispatched Alice to call the other children from the street, and when they came in at one time or another during the visit, introduced them gently and proudly. Alice and Louise remained present throughout the interview. John came in once, grinned at the worker and left immediately afterward. When the worker talked for a minute with the children, Mrs. C seemed glad. After a bit Mrs. C seemed a little less tense, and she said that she was sorry she had to get so excited, but she was a mother, and it was hard. Worker agreed that it was, and said that the agency realized the difficulty in managing on the amount of money given. The clothing list was made out. Although Mrs. C had said at first that all the children needed everything, she was able now to mention specific needs.

In the second example of group interaction, note the use of the first person as a change from earlier conventions. See Chapter VII.

GROUP INTERACTION

Process shown

10-21-37: . . . As I approached, a stoutish young woman, with a little girl wearing thick glasses, came down the steps. The child lagged behind the woman. They were going out, because it was a beautiful day. Nevertheless, she was ready to stop. I felt anxiety in her eagerness to talk—her immediate inference that I had come about Lucy. At first Mrs. B thought I represented the school. When I mentioned the clinic, she became defensive. She hadn't come to clinic because Dr. L was to be away until November. Lucy, who had been watching us suspiciously from a distance, now pulled at her mother's coat, shouting, "Don't tell her. Don't tell the lady!" Then she stood off again and called out resentfully, "You always tell everybody about me." In a controlled conciliatory voice Mrs. B pleaded, "Come, Lucy, be nice to the lady. She's from the school." Lucy remained unfriendly. She repulsed her mother's outstretched hand, made a gesture as if to strike Mrs. B, and said, with intense feeling, "I don't want to be near you. I don't want to go with you!" Helplessly, Mrs. B turned to me and apologized, "She gets that way sometimes. You know—a child— she gets fresh." I could see it was hard for Mrs. B to have a stranger witness the full force of Lucy's behavior. I also felt Mrs. B was testing how much I knew of the whole situation. I suggested I knew a little about Lucy. With some apprehension, Mrs. B asked how I knew. I said casually that I had seen the hospital records and knew some of the last worker's impressions. This helped to put Mrs. B at greater ease, but she continued to be protective of Lucy throughout the interview. Lucy was disturbed by my presence. She kept referring loudly to "the lady" and "the school." Mrs. B whispered to me that Lucy is more friendly towards the school than she is towards the hospital.

As we walked along, Mrs. B talked continuously in a low voice about Lucy. I could see the child edging closer, apparently intensely interested in our conversation. I tried to keep the talk on a superficial level. Mrs. B mentioned that Lucy is really "very smart" and to give the child a feeling of approval, I said, loud enough for her to hear, "Yes she *is* a bright child." I could see Lucy watching me furtively. We came to a street corner, and Lucy objected to holding her mother's hand. I said casually that probably Lucy could walk across beside us without holding hands, just like grown-ups. Lucy responded. She walked stiffly close to her mother, then ran as she neared the other side. Once on the sidewalk she turned to me, bidding for approval. Mrs. B, deep in talk, scarcely noticed, but I said, aloud, "I knew she could do it." After this, Lucy walked along more compliantly.

Mrs. B finds it hard to refuse Lucy anything, and, in doing so, usually offers a promise or a substitute. We came to an opening where there were benches and sat down. Lucy saw a bootblack nearby and demanded a nickel for a shine. She was refused a shine, but Mrs. B acquiesced partly by giving her a few pennies with which to play. Lucy said defiantly she was going to get a shine. Mrs. B loudly forbade her to do this. Mrs. B was tense and had difficulty exercising self-control. She was still trying to impress me—to excuse and minimize Lucy's behavior. Lucy dashed off, Mrs. B watching until she saw Lucy did not intend to get a shine. Then with relief, Mrs. B said, "There, I knew she wouldn't do it. She's afraid when I tell her not to." . . . I commented that Lucy's present difficulty seemed to have more to do with her feelings than with her physical condition. That's why she had been referred to Dr. L who had a special understanding of how children felt and why they acted as they did. Mrs. B . . . recalled the doctor's instructions; she had tried to follow them. She doesn't give in to Lucy as much as before . . .

Lucy had returned by now and began pulling at her mother. Mrs. B urged her to "be nice. Talk nicely to the lady." Lucy bargained. She would talk to "the lady" if she could have my books. I said I couldn't give her my books. She turned to me and spoke directly for the first time, "Why not?" I explained they weren't mine. She made a dramatic gesture of affection towards her mother, putting her arms around Mrs. B's neck and calling her "Mummy." Mrs. B appeared uncomfortable. Lucy turned to me again and said, "I like singing best." I asked if Lucy knew a song about snow. She said, "No." Then, to me, imperiously, "You sing a song." I said I'd like to but I couldn't in the street. I might disturb other people; besides the nearby "L" made too much noise. She insisted that I sing, bargaining again, "If you sing one, I'll sing one." I replied firmly that I could not sing now, but I'd be glad to come again next week and we could sing songs together in the house. She still pleaded, "Just one song, very, very low." I said I couldn't but next week I would in the house. Would she like me to come? She said, "Yes," then ran off.

. . . Lucy came over, and we rose to go. Lucy kept bidding for her mother's attention. She still begged to have her shoes shined . . . We were walking back towards the house now. Lucy, who had been walking on the other side of her mother deftly slipped between Mrs. B and myself. We came to the crossing and I casually took Lucy's hand. She allowed her hand to rest in mine until we were half across the street, then she snatched it away. Nevertheless she came close when I was saying good-bye to Mrs. B. I bent towards Lucy and said, "Then you and I have a date for next week, Lucy, to sing songs." She hesitated, then smiled up at me shyly and said, "Yes." Mrs. B beamed. I said to Lucy, "Shall we shake hands?" She put her hand in mine for a moment. I felt that, despite her persistent negativism, there had been enough evidence of positive reaction from the child to warrant further efforts with her.

Sometimes a summarized period in a record is broken with good effect by an interview reproduced either selectively or in full to show behavior and feeling through the methods already described.

PERIODIC SUMMARY

Approximately six months

Mary is a stocky, dowdy-appearing girl who speaks in a stilted and dignified manner. She still hoped to be a lawyer but thought that this dream could never be realized and that it was practical to think of majoring in social sciences. In a dreamy manner she spoke of her interest in archeology. When the worker commented on her heavy burden she replied that she went out as much as she cared to. Asked what she planned on in September when Charles would be 16 and beyond the age for mother's allowance, she said that she hoped George would have work. She had "a philosophy that since she had gone so far she would continue. If you let matters run things are not so hard to face as you imagine them to be." Smiling, she said that, though it is hard on George, he shouldered it like a man. She hopes he can get work in a radio factory as that is what he is suited for. She spoke warmly of Charles who was always her favorite. He was generous with the money that he earned. Mary was almost as vague as George regarding their financial status, and it became clear that Mrs. W held the purse strings, did the planning, and directed Mary. Because of her school hours it was necessarily felt that George would have to assume the responsibility for discussing relief needs.

George showed great distaste for this. Rather than tell of bills due, he allowed the electric light and gas to be shut off and with difficulty went to the utilities companies with the money given him for the bills. In March, 1935, George became interested in a "white collar job" through WPA.[9] When he realized that the family must go on home

[9] *Works Progress Administration.*

relief in order to be eligible he decided to concentrate on a job in private industry. As nothing materialized in April, he inquired about CCC[10] placement. He spoke more openly of his conflicts with Charles, who had begun to be truant again. He thought that referring Charles to a child guidance clinic might be helpful.

In July George was placed by State Employment Bureau as an elevator operator in a hotel at $50 a month. He stayed four days, asked for his pay, and did not return. He did not reply to a telegram from State Employment asking him to discuss it with them but came to the district office. He said that he had been ill. He had not thought to telephone the hotel. He referred to it as an "unfortunate episode," and spoke of his "rotten luck." He was hopeful, however, that he might find work in a radio station as a technician and had put in his application. He seemed uneasy when speaking of Mary. They all hoped that she could continue with college after her long struggle, but he didn't see how this would be possible. He hoped that soon he would be able to support the whole family. He continued his search, disguising his disappointment, speaking hopefully, yet directing his search along lines that seemed impractical and unpromising.

Charles had been transferred in September to an annex of the F. High School. He did not like this, as there was no school paper. He had absented himself rather frequently. A school visit revealed the interest of the principal and teachers in him, although they could offer him little that would be an incentive to responsibility. Any such posts were awarded boys whose scholarship was excellent. The case worker attempted to find an after-school job for Charles in the office of a neighborhood newspaper. He was not interested in settlement groups. The case worker asked Charles's assistance in escorting a large group of younger boys to the Rodeo. He called for them at their homes and returned them. He was alert and efficient throughout the afternoon. A little negro boy of eight liked Charles so much that he and some neighborhood friends came to the office to ask the case worker if Charles could be their club leader. Charles was delighted with this, secured his probation officer's approval, and arranged with the librarian of

[10] *Civilian Conservation Corps.*

a neighborhood public library to use a vacant room for the club meetings.

Transfer to Relief Bureau in September was discussed with Mary, as the cessation of mother's allowance for Charles was imminent and employment for George through a public works job might be possible. She was told of the Relief Bureau budget, and it was suggested that if they considered moving to a better apartment within the Relief Bureau rent range, it might be an appropriate time to move. Charles's happiness and the cessation of quarreling between the boys seemed to be such satisfying factors that the discomfort of the apartment appeared to be of little concern. George got a few odd jobs repairing radios, but as nothing steady was found he made application. The case had been previously discussed by the family agency with Home Relief Bureau, the investigation was quickly made, and the family accepted the new regime easily. The case was held coöperatively. The family agency planned to continue interest in Charles's school adaptation, his vocational steering, and recreational interests. George was registered both as a clerk and electrician. He spoke hopefully to the case worker of a salary of $90 a month. Later he came in much disturbed because "by mistake" Mary had been called to register at the National Reemployment Service. He didn't want her to work. "It would be a crime for her to stop college." The case worker suggested that on the other hand perhaps it would be very hard for him to face supporting his family alone. He felt that he and Charles did not "deserve so much" as they had never done well in school, whereas Mary had always worked hard to be at the top of her class. He thought that he would try to talk with the investigator to urge him to "forget about Mary's working."

Early in October Mary came to see the case worker. She was pale and disturbed and sat down heavily. "What are we going to do about our rent?" she asked. She regretted now that they had not moved. She could not believe that only $12 could be paid for the present apartment. The electric light bill was far beyond the allowance. She seemed for the first time to realize what the case worker had meant when these things were discussed. She looked up in a dazed fashion. "It's hard to believe that something like this can happen. It has been a nightmare waiting for it to come." She had always thought that somehow she would get through college. If only George had stayed at CCC or had a job, they would not be in this position. The case worker agreed that it would be natural for her to feel bitterly about George's unemployment. She said that she did not feel bitter. She did not blame him for the loss of her college education. Surely both of them would not be expected to work. She was more concerned about her mother, who seemed more helpless and demanding. The case worker asked if it would seem wise to her at this time to consider hospitalizing her mother for treatment at M. She could not think of this. If it were not for her mother's influence the family would break up. It is her love and interest that keeps them together. Charles has begun to play truant again. Before long she felt the probation officer would lose patience. She wept, swaying in her chair, "It is as if this is the very end."

The combination of episodes with occasional quotation and the longer interview may bring out significances in the family interaction. Diagnostic statement or discussion should, however, follow this as other types of summary in order to clarify the picture so presented.

The most famous description in all literature is that of Helen's beauty, in which the dynamic effect of her appearance on the old men who are standing on the walls of Troy is given. Thus to create an emotional effect through interaction and context might be an argument for process as the highest type of recording. But after all we are dealing with a professional record, not literature, and cost, if no other factor, would force us into experimentation with different mediums to try to convey the significance of the social-personal situation. The social worker has to consider a social situation, as well as the introspection of the patient; the social worker holds relatively few consecutive interviews over relatively short periods of time; the social worker deals with foreground or immediate emotional material as over against the deeper layers of emotional life, and for all these reasons the social worker needs to keep proportion with respect to the importance of context and sequence in the recorded interview. Professor Whitehead in his *Adventures of Ideas* says, "The success of language in conveying information is vastly overrated, especially in learned circles . . . The general truth of Hume's doctrine as to the necessity of first-hand impressions is inexorable." There are limitations inherent in any form of record, which we must accept. The reader will see for himself the unmanageability of such long entries as those cited in this chapter and can be his own editor. There is no easy way of learning to shorten records, and in the field of social and psychological values records will for many years reflect our flounderings and adventures. Meanwhile we must always remember the administrative setting, the community attitudes, and the limitations of our own competence so that most records will be simple and concise and only a small number will be chosen for experimentation.

We should not assume too readily that different types of content require a definite art form to carry them. We do say that executive treatment and services as well as clean-cut and well-understood interpretive procedures may be either summarized or indicated and need not be reproduced. But this would not always be so. And we do say that a group interaction or worker-client therapy is not easily indicated without reproducing a good deal of behavior and conversation, but this is not final. Again we come back to the observation that the interpretation or diagnostic insistence of the highly-trained worker can reduce the necessity for bulk factual material of all kinds, although it can never replace the need for sufficient concrete factual and behavioristic (including lingual behavior) material in the record. Selection in the recording of process as selection in all other recording tends to increase the likelihood of a significant document.

VII

STYLE

MANY writers of records are interested in such arrangements of detail as commonly are thought to make up style. A professional style is as elusive in case records as is style in a sonnet or letter or a novel, because "style" is a shorthand word for expressing a complex of behavior, emotion, and thought. Good usage, good grammar, good construction of sentences and paragraphs are the basis of all style, but the professional record cannot quite follow Barrett Wendell's principles of unity, mass, and coherence. Life is too inconsistent and treatment usually too opportunistic for logical records. Yet the fact that each case is a sort of abstraction, a professionally conceived unit of elements which we feel relevant to us, does make for some unity. The meaning of a case for us professionally emerges as it progresses, so that our grasp of significance is dynamic rather than ultimate, practical rather than theoretical. A good professional style must mean that back of it is a good diagnostician or there will be no problem-solving unity. A sense of significance must be greater rather than less in the recording of process in relationship treatment or the whole is an unreadable hodge-podge.

Questions concretely raised about style have to do with tense, person, phrasing, use of slang, professional terminology, beheaded sentences (subject omitted), elliptical sentences, and so on. Tense should, of course, follow ordinary grammatical rules, the point being raised because of the practice of putting treatment in the present tense, e.g., "worker asks (asked) Mrs. Smith if she would like to go to the country"; "worker visits (visited) the Jenkins family, finds (found) Jimmy at home alone"; "Mr. Brown replies (replied) that he was deeply upset." Some recorders select the present tense because it seems a more vivid or dramatic tense. But this very practice makes it more difficult to sustain for routine events, and writers often slip back into the narrative past without noticing the shift. For this reason the past tense is probably preferable.[1]

For a long time persons on the face sheet and in the text were referred to as 1—2—3—4—5—that is, one was the man, two the woman, and the children were numbered thereafter. Later this yielded to man, woman, child, and now the accepted usage is "Mr. Brown," "Mrs. Brown," and "Tommy"; with, however, the usual alternations of "mother," "father," "foster mother," "sister," as called for.[2]

[1] Readers may have been troubled by the loose sentence structure and poor English shown in many of the illustrations. Those persons who have not learned how to write before leaving college will not learn in a professional school, and even those with good style may fall into careless habits under the conditions of hasty dictation and transcription prevailing in most agencies. Little editing, other than what was necessary to disguise material, has been attempted in this text. Professional method and content have been the sole considerations in choosing illustrations.

[2] A committee asked to comment for the writer on present usages in a large public welfare agency reported as follows: We refer to the clients as Mr. or Mrs. A, or Miss B, rather than by the terms M and W or the client's first name. Children are referred to by their name rather than by such expressions as "the youngest" or "the oldest." When other individuals are mentioned in the record they are referred to by their full surnames. The date of the visit appears in the margin and is repeated at the beginning of each new entry even though there are a number of visits made on the same date. This is preferred to such expressions as "later" or "same day." The place of the interview, whether at the home or office, and the persons interviewed need to be made clear.

The use of the third person is common, although there is a current leaning to the first person plural ("we said," "we suggested," "it occurred to us," "we wondered if," even, with a touch of absurdity, "we smiled as we sat down"). The "we" style seems to lend itself pleasantly to material in which there is parenthetical diagnostic impression or comment by the worker as in the following:[3]

Mrs. F is always looking for symptoms, and visitor wonders whether the hospital experience has affected Roland in any way or whether he is just becoming a nuisance in the neighborhood and is suffering more from disapproval than formerly . . . Mrs. F has sometimes noted anger and rage on his face, but if he sees that she notices, his face becomes a blank and he pretends that he isn't angry. Mrs. F asked visitor whether she thought the treatment at the clinic was making him behave like this. Visitor said that sometimes the behavior of children under this treatment became worse for a time before it improved. Visitor is not sure whether it was wise to say this to Mrs. F, because if Roland becomes unruly in the future, she may blame it on the clinic visits. However, we had to give her some explanation, and the immediate effect was to make her more reconciled . . . When Mrs. F asked the visitor what we would have done, visitor tried to avoid seeming critical and did not wish to commit ourselves to specific advice, which might be followed on another occasion. We said it would seem wise, when there was every indication that Roland was in a disturbed mood, not to press the matter of doing his lessons or to raise any issue with him which could be avoided. Also we said we thought it was too bad that Mrs. F had struggled to undress him when he might as easily have stayed there dressed until he felt like undressing himself as it just prolonged what seemed to Roland a contest of wills. However, visitor added, we probably could not have handled the situation nearly so well as Mrs. F had. We told her what the doctor had said and gave her the encouragement that if she could endure Roland's behavior for a while longer in all likelihood he would get over it and be a happier and

[3] In current usage "case worker" is preferred to "visitor" or "agent."

healthier boy. We did not ask her to keep Roland, but we could see that as the conversation progressed she was changing her mind in this respect.

Until recently convention has been against the use of the first person, although it has been used for some years for comment in much the same way as the first person plural, above; now many records are written in the first person throughout. "I think May is feeling more secure in foster mother's affections"; "I believe man's evasion as to work history and his extreme resentment against the police and the system suggest that we should allow for the possibility of a prison record." Consultants' and supervisors' notes may be written in the first person and signed. Comments should not be too frequent, but their very nature permits a little more freedom than the formal evaluation.

Letters from one agency to another properly employ the "we" editorial style, but unless carefully watched this may give an authoritative, patronizing, or pompous effect. Thus: "We are writing you to secure information about the parents' present situation." "We think that he should be committed to Vineland." (Compare: "Do you not think that he should . . . ?") "Our plan for Ruth, who is experienced in housework and seems devoted to her baby, is to find her after a period of convalescence such a position with her child." (Compare: "Would you agree that Ruth should . . . ?") "Mrs. E has shown an increasing tendency to withdraw from her relationship with us, so that we feel unable at this time to help with such problems as connecting the children with more adequate recreational facilities. Our willingness to reopen the case would depend on the nature of their request for help, which at present seems to be relief for the family and shelter for Mr. E's feelings."

A simple natural style is not dependent on the person used, but in the next illustration the use of the first person, the choice of detail, and the question, "would you permit us?" rather than the declarative form, "we feel that he should be placed in the hospital," all play into the persuasive effect of the whole. The excerpt from a letter to the Superintendent of the Poor, reads as follows:

> For the last few days I have been trying to run down the parentage of the above-named child, Buster Berrien, but thus far I have not heard from my inquiries. However, I still have hope!
>
> Mrs. Martin, the boarding mother, thought the child was diseased, but I had a blood test made and just yesterday the report came in saying it was negative. A uranalysis was also made, and this was reported negative, but for some reason or other the child is very much undernourished and is exceptionally thin and anemic. He seems bright and normal mentally. This morning I went to Dr. Wilson's office and talked with him about the child. He suggests that the chap be placed in the Radcliffe Hospital under his care for a month or two to see what can be done to build him up. Dr. Wilson will give his services, but the hospital bill will be an item, of course. If the child could only get built up, I have no doubt but that he would be very placeable in a foster home; but as it is, his future is dubious.
>
> Would you permit me to place him in the hospital as a county charge for a while to see how he develops, or would you care to make some other suggestions?

The words and phrases used in records, more than the person, determine whether the style is formal or informal, dignified or decorated. A simple, direct, lucid style is always to be preferred. Probation and court records have shown a tendency to legal phraseology and sometimes to overelaborate diction. The present trend in court records is away from legalistic terminology to plain English, and with all records the swing is away from psychiatric word borrowings. "Foreign" words or phrases borrowed from psychiatry and medicine may be employed only if they have been thoroughly naturalized in social work: "She herself has a somewhat rigid attitude, answers questions with simply 'yes' or 'no,' does not talk spontaneously, has a frank expressionless *facies*, and talks in a monotonous way." The word *facies* here is to be questioned as would be "libidinal security," "cathexis," "narcissism," if other words can be substituted without loss of sense. That the foreign, or imported, word is all too frequently overworked does not add to its charm. Sometimes lack of real knowledge of the subject leads to absurdities like: "He never indulged in sex relations as he is conflicted over the sexual act. There are indications of an Oedipus complex and schizophrenia. Fortunately printing is his trade, and in this he found sublimation."

Ugly formations of words like "referrals" or "to contact" are in such common use that they may be good usage soon. In letters between social agencies we should be careful to use technical words and phrases only if they have wide and common professional status, and in letters to laymen we should not even use these.

Description of behavior or incident is so much a part of all records that illustration is difficult. One can only say that some of it is better than others. The red cloth on the piano and the baby cooing in the carriage may be expanded into such trivialities as:

All the conversation was very friendly, and the occasion tended to be too festive to pretend to do much more than establish a friendly interest in the family. As worker had a definite engagement, she announced the necessity of leaving after the spaghetti had been consumed. They would not hear of it, and would not let her move. Worker diverted their attention by calling attention to the victrola, and the children immediately turned it on. Mr. N got out a guitar and played with the victrola. He has a mandolin, which is very old and needs repairing. By constant insistence it was finally possible to get coat and hat, and just as worker was leaving Josie came running in with a box from the pastry shop. They explained that they had not wanted to buy a dessert until they knew the worker would be there, so Josie had slipped out after eating her spaghetti to buy the pastry. They would not let the worker leave without taking the box, saying it was just a couple of little cakes. After much protesting it seemed necessary to take the box which, it was later discovered, contained 6 large chocolate eclairs.

Surely a single sentence might have served for the entire description. A better-trained eye and ear give us the following:

Mrs. I sews all the children's clothes, patches and mends until things can no longer be used, does all her shopping on Tenth Avenue and in the chain stores and from vegetable stands. She plans and buys in such a way that she always knows meals in advance what they will have because she uses all the left-overs. She also closely watches the sales, buying her soap only when she can get six cakes at a special price. She never buys on credit. The family always sits down to a set table.

The use of incidents may be effective:

From a closet in the bedroom Mrs. I brought out a dusty bag from which she took a stuffed and mended parrot. Laura was always a family pet and "was fussed over as if she were a child." When Mrs. I came back from the hospital when Jeannette was born, the parrot was brokenhearted. She refused to eat and finally died, Mrs. I says, of grief and jealousy.

Mrs. I was so deeply moved by the loss of the parrot that her breast milk was affected.

As Mr. S signed the voucher he said, "You see me five years ago. Got a job, I happy. I no work too hard. Just work with hands, not body. I come home, I eat, I satisfied. Me young man then, now old." And he passed his hands through the air in a little hopeless gesture. Then carefully Mr. S took from a back pocket a newspaper-wrapped tool. He uncovered it and carefully explained its use. Suddenly he stopped cutting imaginary pocketbooks from the desk blotter and smiled shamefacedly as he replaced and rewrapped the tool.

The directly quoted interview can be both effective and important, as we have seen in Chapter VI, and may be particularly useful in bringing out treatment.

She had been very small then and could not remember exactly when it was or just how long they had stayed. Most of the time she had spent with her mother. "I didn't have as much chance of getting spoiled as Andrew. I guess there's always one in every family that is spoiled." Mrs. W laughed, "Well, in our family, it wasn't me; it was my brother." Worker asked Mrs. W what she meant by being spoiled. "You know, there's the little things they get instead of you. I can understand it now, but I couldn't then. You don't see things the same way when you are a little child as you do when you grow up. I didn't understand. I got mad at my mother and father too sometimes. But now I can see that they didn't like each other and they didn't like me either. That is, my mother didn't like me. You see my mother was married before. My brother was a son by her first husband. I know she loved her first husband much better than she loved my father. I looked like my father. Every time she looked at me she had to think of my father. It made her not like me, because I reminded her of him. But I couldn't see all this then. It made me mad; I wanted to slap her; I wanted to hit my brother; I wanted to run away. I did get into lots of trouble. I was always a tomboy. They said I was bad. I know now that you have to hate just the same as you have to love. You can't have everything all the time. My mother couldn't help it because she hated me. It had to come out somewhere, the feeling was there, and it came out on me." Mrs. W continued speaking of the "little things" that her brother seemed to get that she didn't get. If there was one bicycle it was for him. If they had enough money to buy clothes for one of them, her brother got the clothes.

An example of a mixed style with direct and indirect quotation freely used is in the following:

Worker asked him smilingly what other troubles he had. With some irritation and yet with a rather petulant tone of voice he said he had a problem. (Can you tell me about it?) "I feel so guilty because I can't work. Gee, my mother has supported me long enough. All I do is sleep and eat." He thinks only of success—he would like to be a big executive, like a president or vice-president, say of some silk concern or other big business. (How could you attain this?) "Oh, I could attain this through stenography." This last was said haltingly and in a mumbling tone of voice. (Do you think a great deal about all this?) "Yes, and I like to read biographies and success stories." David changed the subject to say that his father believes in hard work. He has good parents. They have pleasant meals at home, though his mother has to cook after a hard day's work at the pushcart. Still he recalls that he worked very hard as a child. He shoved his coat over, placed his hand on his right shoulder and said, "Many is the time I carried 50 pounds of wood on this shoulder. No, my parents never asked me to work hard, but I did all I could to help. I carried heavy loads of wood for a kid of my size; I worked hard. Isn't it a shame I can't find work now? I feel very guilty because I can't find work." (Is anything else on your mind?) "Yes, I want my brother to be a success." He then told how he assumed a parental rôle in the family, bosses his brother and sister. He urges them to do their homework, to go to school on time, and to do their work. (What happens when they don't do as you wish?) "Sometimes I get nervous and hit them, and sometimes I tell them I wish someone had been there to push me when I was younger." He went on to tell that his father is getting old and nervous. When he is not at the hospital "he sits at the stand with my mother. They talk like love birds. You ought to see my parents—how happy they are together. I tell you, they are just like love birds. Believe me, I can tell the difference when I visit my boy friends' homes

—their parents are not as happy as mine." Here he digressed to speak in an animated voice and in an approving manner of what a fine business woman his mother is and she is a clever linguist—speaks about seven languages.

The device of parentheses used here for the worker's questions and comments becomes tiring to the eye if they appear in great quantity through successive pages.

When large blocks of material are quoted, no devices seem to make an easily-read page. The completely unbroken paragraph presents about as many difficulties as the use of italics and parentheses.

He can't keep on doing everything his father wants him to. There was a time when he did whatever his mother wanted in the house, washing windows, scrubbing floors, and housework. With a good deal of anger he says he can't do that now. He would do it even if the boys did see him. Still, he feels it isn't right. Fellows all tell him that he's twenty, and they want to know why he doesn't answer his father back, but he can't seem to. He tells of Colgero who fights his father back. Collie hits and answers him. But he can't seem to do that. We asked if he has any idea as to why he can't. It just isn't in him. He still honors his father. The other day he was talking to his father and he said in English "will you" which means something dirty in Italian, and his father started to beat him up. His mother had to explain that it was English and that it didn't mean anything dirty. Then he shakes his head sadly and says that he just can't talk to his father. They all speak Italian in his house anyway, and his father doesn't understand any English. His father is not like anybody else. He still thinks he is in Italy. We wonder if any of the boy's friends or cousins have the same trouble. He shakes his head; no, none of them. Why, even in the matter of this suit he is wearing, he didn't want it, but his mother made him get it. He doesn't like brown and wanted an oxford grey suit. His father picked his hat and shoes for him. He gives us some of the details of this. We wonder in this instance why he felt that he couldn't assert his own wishes. He doesn't know. His mother told him that an oxford grey suit was too light, so he just let her go ahead. We remark that it is hard, isn't it, as you grow up to have to accept responsibility for your own decisions, so that if you buy a suit, for example, and it doesn't wear well, then you have to take all the blame. He nods, seems to agree with this, says also it is his father's money he is spending, that his father always tells him that. His father asks who should say how he spends his money. We ask when he first started having trouble with his father. When he was about 15. He started to want to do things for himself—that was about the time he started growing up. We say these problems do start coming up then. After all, his father and mother had taken care of him and sort of protected him until that time, but it is hard to break away to be able to make your own decisions. It's something like a baby that has to be weaned gradually from its mother. He nods again at this and agrees.

Beginning each speaker's remark on a fresh line makes reading easier but is wasteful of space. Paragraphing in this type of recording must be arbitrary, but at least some breaking up of the close packed effect in the last sample should be attempted. The best solution is that of selectivity in the choice of interviews to be so fully reproduced, and of material within interviews. During the period of extensive use of verbatim reproduction, the awkwardness of which is undeniable for general use, marginal indexing, parentheses, italics, indentation, and frequent breaking up of the solid page, all afford, if not overelaborated, some relief to the eye.

The next illustration shows in straightforward sentences, but with arbitrary paragraphing, treatment process. Style and content seem harmoniously designed to show the movement in the interviews although the brief excerpt given reveals this incompletely. Other examples are found in the preceding chapter. In the

recording of interviewing process "the style" is most
particularly "the man."

Alice at office. Worker got the impression that Alice was not
interested in discussing these things and felt that the interview
should not break off at this point. We asked whether John
were enrolled for the fall quarter at college. Alice said that he
was. She told about a contractor who was trying to get him
some odd job as a helper. John hasn't done much work of this
sort.

There was again a pause which worker did not break. Alice
said that things were pretty bad sometimes, but she thinks she
ought not to complain. There are people worse off than she
is. At least, when she gets in a jam she can come in here and
we will help her. Worker said that there were lots of things
that Alice "was in a jam" about that we didn't help with.
Alice said that that was so. She went on to say that you should
think of the people who are worse off and more miserable
than you. Worker said perhaps, but one usually doesn't think
that way—rather of how much better off other people are.
Alice agreed to that. She said she couldn't help thinking of
unpleasant things.

It was suggested by worker that sometimes, too, Alice would
not feel like coming in. Alice said that wasn't it. If she let
herself be guided by her feelings she would never do anything. Therefore, she makes it her business to do what she
has to do. Worker said that it was hard for Alice to come in,
and we realized that. Alice said, now, that this was so. The
family left everything to her—all the responsibility was on
her shoulders, even coming in here. Sometimes she just didn't
want to take it. She wanted to do just as she pleased sometimes. Worker said that Alice did carry the family responsibilities and that we'd left things up to her too. Alice nodded
but made no comment. Worker wasn't certain that this remark had reached her.

She then stated rather abruptly that she must be going. She
asked about the appointment for next week. Worker stated
several times when she would be available. However, worker
suggested that Alice might decide herself whether she wished
to come in next week. If she preferred not to, worker would
understand about it, and Alice could let her know about the
money she would need. Alice smiled and said, "All right."

The record continues with a slightly different arrangement to indicate rôles.

Alice at office. She seems to enunciate less distinctly in the beginning of the interview. She started out by saying, "So you saw my brother. What did you think of him? Was it as I said?" Worker said yes, John had been in. Alice said, "Do you think he wants to work? Do you think you can help him to get a job?" Worker said that we had given him a card to register with our employment worker. *Alice:* "He wanted me to ask you something, but I told him I had to ask things for myself." There was some indication in her tone that it wasn't as hard to ask any more. She went on, "Anyway, he can just learn to ask for things for himself. He's old enough. He knows the way down here." Her mother wanted her to ask for him. Alice told her what she thought. *Worker:* "What did you tell her? *Alice:* "Plenty." After a pause she said, "He told you something that wasn't true. He said that he didn't want to tell you that he was doing nothing, so he told you about delivering for a grocer. Maybe he'll have to come to that some day." She went on in her usual vein about the fact that he will have to learn some day, that he will never work, that she's going to stand it just one year more, and that if she were earning the way she used to she would leave now. She repeated that he wanted her to ask worker something, but she wouldn't do it. She elaborated on this for some time. There were more pauses in her talk than in previous interviews. Worker felt that Alice's refusal to voice her brother's request was inhibiting her. Finally worker had a chance to say suppose her brother were working, would she be any happier? Alice started to say perhaps not, then caught herself, and said, "I know him too well. That will never happen." She gave some details of other people's attitude toward John, that is her cousin's and her girl friend's. They all see how things are at home. The implication is that they all blame John and don't see how she stands it. Alice said the one peaceful time she remembers was when John was working in South America. She never gave him a thought. Worker said that she wasn't sure that she quite believed that. Alice said, "You better believe it." Worker said, "Were you ever happy?" Alice repeated, "Was I ever happy?" *Worker:* "Were you happy as a child?"

"I didn't think about it," said Alice. Suddenly she began to cry, and said in a sort of explosive tone, "I remember my father." Worker repeated, "You remember your father?" *Alice:* "Yes." She began crying more openly. "If he had lived things wouldn't be like this." *Worker:* "You miss him very much?" *Alice:* "Don't let us go into that now please."

During the next part of the interview she kept her handkerchief in front of her face and found it difficult to talk. After a brief pause worker said: "How old were you when he died?" *Alice:* "I was almost five." *Worker:* "Was there anyone to love you after that?" *Alice:* "My grandmother. She died. She died when I was eleven." *Worker:* "It was hard for you to be left alone twice." *Alice:* "My mother left me and my brother for my aunt to take care of, and my aunt always liked my brother best, I didn't know it then." She added inconsistently, "But children are always right about such feelings." *Worker:* "You felt very much alone. When did your mother leave?" *Alice:* "My mother left right after my father died. She had her plans all made beforehand. This was her second trip to Europe. She went once when she was single. She went for her health. She stayed three years." Pause. "The only good thing my aunt has ever said about me is that I can take care of myself. That makes me feel very much alone." *Worker:* "It is pleasanter to be taken care of."

Another interview shows the same concentration on the interplay of behavior and remarks, which we have alluded to frequently as the recording of process. This reversion to the informal style of conversation is introduced in the given illustration into the middle of a formal summary. Evidently the worker regarded the expression of feeling as important and showed it this way rather than through diagnostic comment.

Mr. C had come in to see us after we had talked with Mrs. C about our not seeing him. During the interview, as in previous interviews, he seemed quite jumpy and somewhat embarrassed, although he made an obvious effort to be composed. He greeted worker quite elaborately, bowed to her, shaking hands, asking her how she was feeling and how she had been getting along. Worker asked how things had been for him. Mr. C said that as far as his work was concerned, he still wasn't earning a great deal of money.

He then expressed appreciation for the suit that we had given him, saying that the men with whom he had worked said that it was a $60 suit. It looked very well on him, and he wanted to thank us a lot. He looked up at worker and said with feeling, "You do so much for us. You've been so nice to us all the time." Worker commented on the fact that he felt so strongly about it, and we wondered why. He was a little embarrassed at this. Said that it was just because we had been so very nice to him. Worker said that sometimes people found it hard to accept other people being nice to them. They felt that they shouldn't take so much. He made no direct response to this, merely fidgeting around, then looked up and asked worker if she was happy, saying that he hoped that we were very happy in our married life just because we had been so nice. He hopes some day we have a family too. He continued saying that it's very nice for someone to have a family. He knows how much he loves his family. His face sobered. He spoke with feeling as he said that he missed his children a great deal.

He suddenly said, "You know Arlene is not my child, but you're the only one that I've ever told about it." Worker said that once before he had told us this. We wondered why he felt that he had to tell us about it and why it meant so much to him. Mr. C said well he didn't talk about it because everybody else thought that it was his child. It was his first wife's child by a former marriage; then after her husband died he married her. He hadn't known her first husband, but he knew that he had been very sick and that he had left her a widow with this one child. He had never told anybody about it, however, because he has some wealthy relatives, Germans, who live in New Jersey. They are very well off and educated. They might think that there was something funny about his marrying a widow, but he has always told them that it was his child and that he had married his wife after the child was born. They believe it and have never said anything more about it. Worker asked him why he thought they might have some feeling about his marrying a widow. He was somewhat embarrassed at this and said it's because he was younger than his wife, and they would think that it was funny for him to make that kind of a marriage. He paused and worker said, "Maybe you felt a little funny too about marrying a widow." He wriggled around in his chair, laughed in an embarrassed fashion, and said that he did at first because he was younger, but she was such a good woman that it was all right, and he really considered Arlene as his own child. He changed the subject abruptly at this point and brought out a dispossess.

A form of case presentation is next shown which has the features of full verbatim reproduction of the worker's rôle, the use of the first person singular, and a sentence or two of diagnostic comment or interpretation. Although records cannot and should not be written so fully except for occasional study purposes the style (process) is here used in appropriate material with simplicity and effectiveness. See Chapter VI.

Mrs. J in District Office promptly at 12:00.[4] She extended her hand in greeting, "I'm so glad you are going to be my worker. I was very anxious about it."

We were both standing; I asked her to sit down. She sat, leaning her elbows on the desk, her body tense and erect. She pushed herself as much forward as was possible, her eyes full of tears which she struggled and managed to control. Her face changed color from extreme paleness to deep blush.

"I had a little trouble the last few weeks. I want to tell you about it, and I'm ashamed of talking, as it is hard."

I agreed, "Yes, it is very hard to talk to a new person."

She smiled, "You understand; Miss M said you would. I asked that you be my worker, but Miss M said she couldn't promise. She said she would try. I didn't want to talk to anybody else in the office. I don't feel that you're a stranger because you made a visit to my house."

"Yes," I said, "I remember."

"Did Miss M tell you," she asked, "about the money?"

"Well no," I said, "I had no conversation with her before she left."

[4] This extract is abridged from the illustration in Miss Beatrice Wajdke's paper, "An Intensive Treatment Approach," in *Differential Approach in Case Work Treatment*, Family Welfare Association, 1936.

"She asked me to tell you that I need money for papering the house. It is in a disgraceful condition. My husband tore it off and didn't finish. He's always like that, starting something and not finishing. He can't get through anything. Do you think it is right for him to be like that?"

"Well, now," I said, "I don't know, Mrs. J."

"That's what I thought; I was afraid you wouldn't understand. Miss M thought that you might."

"Well, now," I said, "it is very hard for you to talk to me, I know, because I am new to you, but perhaps if you try to tell me I may be able to understand; perhaps we both will." . . .

"Yes," she said, "and I got my husband arrested, something I couldn't make up my mind to do before, not that I didn't try. I had him at Municipal Court, but every time I went in to make a complaint I took him back because I thought, 'What's the use?' I didn't like to talk to the probation officers. All they'd say to me was, 'Mrs. J, you're better off than many others; you better put up with it,' but this time I thought, 'before he goes away with that woman I'll have him locked up.'"

"And keep him safe," I said, "so that he could not desert as Miss M did?"

She followed the interview with unusual clearness, though now and then she showed marked surprise. . . .

"Do you think that's why I got Mr. J arrested?"

"Well, now, I don't know. Did you?"

"To think of it, I might have. I was going to the court today to start a case against him for support of the two younger ones. I couldn't get nothing for Mary and Harry because they are over age, but they would give me an order for the two younger ones, except that it wouldn't do any good; but still if I felt that he had to give it to me, I'd feel better even if he doesn't have the money and doesn't work because I am afraid of being left without any help." . . .

I asked, "Need you make a decision right away, now that you know a little about your feeling and how it was all mixed up between Miss M and Mr. J?"

"Oh, you mean that I wanted to keep her here?"

"Well, yes," I said. "You did, didn't you?"

"I hated to have her go," this with a good deal of feeling.

"Yes, you felt that both of them would leave you, so you had one of them arrested."

"I think I will wait a couple of days. When I get my house all fixed up, I would like you to come and see it. Will you come?"

I said, "Well, I make very few visits. Most people come here."

"Well, shall I come next week at the same time?"

"If you like."

"No," she said. "That isn't a good hour for me. I have to get lunch ready. Could I phone you and make an appointment when I see when it is convenient?"

I said, "It would probably be better if we made a tentative appointment now. I will keep the hour for you," naming the hour.

She relegated to me the rôle of the mother—"You buy the shoes." The disappointment which she expressed when I did not serve her in the capacity of the previous worker was the way in which she expressed her anger . . .

In contemporary records parenthetical impressions and inferences from the first intake interview on are common. Obviously except in the hands of a trained worker these may be trivial.

2-11-35.—Mr. M in office for Mrs. M's appointment. He walked slowly into the interviewing room. He sat down holding his hat in his hand and twirled it about. It was worker's impression that he was both nervous and timid. We smiled and waited for him to begin. He said that Mrs. M was ill and putting his hand to his throat indicated that that was the area in which the trouble lay. As the interview progressed his language difficulty became more and more evident. He gave the impression of having prepared a few statements in advance. When he had exhausted these, he had difficulty in conversing. He said the doctor had been in. There had been medicine, various expenses. He was out of a job. He didn't know what to do. She was sleeping in her mama's apartment, very unwell. Times were difficult. The job in the church was good. There were no jobs now. We indicated that we were sorry Mrs. M was not well and that he must be worried. He nodded and smiled and stopped twirling his hat. As if to reassure us he said that she was better now. She will be upstairs soon.

In response to our comment that he would be less worried then, he looked confused. It was not possible to tell whether he did or did not understand. He made it evident that they would need money and we nodded and made out a voucher.

An unusual form of diagnostic statement sets off the client's statements as findings to support the interpretation. It is made effective by a sort of antiphonal arrangement.

Miss C is a young Porto Rican girl, bereft of her mother at the age of eleven, alone in this country, unemployed, without resources, seeking an escape in ill health.

She wants to be taken care of, wants a mother. She indicates her need to be cared for in the first words she says, and she repeats it again and again. Her need for a mother is so great that she literally forces the rôle upon each succeeding worker. With the loss of the preceding worker, it is as if her mother had died again. Her physical symptoms recur with the change of workers, and subside again as she feels more secure.

"I was never really happy without my mother." "Every step of my life I think of her." "The years may run, but I will never forget her." "I want my mother."[5]

She rejects the thought of marriage—marriage would only bring her more troubles. She identifies strongly with her mother and rejects her father and stepfather as causes of her mother's unhappiness and death.

"There may be good men, but I have never seen any."

She does not want to work—wants to be taken care of. She becomes ill when work is mentioned. Her physical symptoms increase. She feels guilty about not working. "I guess there is no real reason why I shouldn't look for work. It isn't nice for a young girl to depend upon others. I ought to be able to take care of myself."

---

[5] In the original material, the client's expression is put in indirect discourse, thus: "She's not stupid, she knows she has heart trouble. Maybe they just don't want her to know, or maybe they don't know enough to find out what is the matter with her. The way she is feeling now she wonders whether anybody will be able to help her." But since it seemed confusing without some device like italics, the client's part has been transposed into the first person.

She feels guilty about accepting relief. She finds an escape from working and a solution for her need to be taken care of in becoming ill. She is unable to accept the hospital's report that there is nothing the matter with her because of her need to escape into illness.

"I hate to come here. I have difficulty breathing when I come. I have palpitation of the heart. I cannot be expected to work if I am sick. I think I may drop dead any time. I feel as if I may fall down. I am dizzy. I have heart trouble."

In having heart trouble she again identifies with her mother. Her feeling that she looks like an old woman may be part of her rejection of marriage and child bearing and may be part of her identification with her mother. The fact that her mother died in childbirth probably ties up with Miss C's rejection of marriage.

There is very little to say about slang except to repeat the caution of those most persuasive grammarians, the brothers Fowler,[6] that slang is meant to be spoken, not written. The practice of quoting interviews verbatim has brought this problem acutely to the front. Here good taste and a sense of what is significant must be the control. A three-page interview with an ex-convict is interlaced with such quotations as:

He doesn't like him and he might tell us that Mr. D is a bad guy. And what if he does? He'd go over and smash his face in, that's what . . . No, Mr. D hates his guts, that's all, and we can tell Goucher so over the phone . . . He hates that lousy work . . . He really does need help now. He owes his landlady. All right, he doesn't say we should pay for that, but he needs help with food at least. Otherwise he'll have to beat it and let the l.l. take the rap, if we can't help him . . . Listen, girlie, there are some things you just can't tell—you can't tell everything. You can make me out a liar if you want to.

One questions the value of this conversation. It is hard to know when the slang quoted is deliberately chosen

[6] Fowler, H. W. and F. T., *The King's English*.

as the best means of revealing a client's attitude or when the writer is tempted by the vigorous and picturesque, as in the preceding quotation. If the reader's attention is directed to the style rather than to the content in a professional record, it is probably an indication of weakness. The following examples illustrate writing for effect with repartee.

When asked what he had done with the money he said, "Did you ever roll the bones? Well, that's where the money went."

Mr. F in office by appointment. He is an extremely corpulent middle-aged man, well dressed and decidedly business-like in his manner. He greeted us brusquely, adding, as he eased himself into a chair, that we were ten minutes late. Without preliminaries he plunged into a discussion of what he came for—the placement of three-year-old Rose Marie. He said with some show of disgust that he had come in about six months ago with the same request, but "that girl fooled around so long that I got plumb sick of it. Now I want to know where I stand this time. If you can put the kid somewhere, say so. If you can't, I'll go elsewhere." As Mr. F glared at us, we said that our business was a little different from his own (Horn and Hardart's Automat), that we couldn't put a nickel in the slot and produce a home exactly suited to the needs of a particular child. Mr. F smiled and with somewhat better grace, almost good naturedly, asked what it was we wanted to know.

Sometimes the writer seems to like slang for its own sake. The next excerpt, obviously from a young writer's record, can hardly be defended.

Visitor lapsed from professional ethics and hit the ceiling. R listened a minute and said gleefully, "Gee, you certainly do have a temper all your own, don't you?" Visitor grinned and replied, "I certainly seem to, but usually I don't lose it, except with you. Now why is that?" R said, "Well, I don't think you would get mad at me if you didn't like me and think I was like—well, like an equal. If you did not care, you would not get mad."

Sometimes quoted material, though unobjectionable, adds little.

The week end went very well on the whole, although Douglas got the impression that he was being "watched" inasmuch as the mother called the children back to her occasionally when out walking, which caused Douglas to say to his mother several times that no dirtiness had gone on this week end whatever.

Equally adequate might have been the sentence: "Douglas has not been engaging in sex play this week." But the choice of either expression would depend on the context and other material given and whether the child's own selection of phrase was important.

"The New York newspapers of October 16 published juicy excerpts from the inmate's letters to Mrs. Elliman."

Here "juicy" has less value than the phrase "no dirtiness" above.

Although we need not be inhibited from giving precise material which, whether pleasant or unpleasant, reveals important motivation, it is the young worker usually who repeats unnecessary intimacies, particularly those of a sex nature, which, in direct quotation, often are vulgarisms. We have accustomed ourselves[7] to this in interviews on sex behavior when the person's own choice of words and concept may be significant, but we should take care that our selection is appropriate to the uses of the record.

[7] Isaacs, Susan, *Social Development in Young Children,* Harcourt Brace, 1933. This gives the behavior and conversations of children in a way and for a purpose that cannot be offensive to the serious reader, and child guidance records habitually record such material so plainly and simply that it is unobtrusive.

Like slang, criticism of coöperating agencies and persons is better not written, and if it must be written should be as factual and objective as possible. One is safer with careful description here than with adjectives and adverbs. Agency relations outlast most workers' individual contacts with them, and current impressions may serve only to caricature some incident.

The objection to such a comment as that quoted below is that, although it may quite well be true, it leaves in the memory a distasteful impression which can not be erased even after workers and program have been changed.

Mrs. P said that she had gone to the Church Institute, where they told her that they couldn't help her. She said that the man there had told her, "A lot of nerve coming to us! Let the Home Relief Bureau give you what you need!"

If the criticism is flavored with patronage or sarcasm, the comment is no more endearing.

Miss Small impressed the probation officer on first meeting as being a frustrated and neurotic individual. Apparently from her mispronunciation of the terms commonly used by a psychiatrist or a more modern educator, one would think that this was the first psychiatric report she had seen. The probation officer made no headway whatever. Upon leaving she thanked Miss Small for revealing so plainly the cause of Angelo's misconduct.

Such terms as "grateful," "antagonistic," "uncoöperative," and so forth, involve a discussion of attitudes as well as recording. Here again the use of quotations or a description of behavior is more effective than phrases which are, in effect, a "label." One of the most confusing questions for a young worker is whether or not to put into the record those things which the client tells him "personally." This problem is involved in the worker's relationship with the client, as well as in the matter of recording. One wonders whether the information which the worker hesitates to record should have been secured from the client. The worker may think that achieving personal liking from the client is an end in itself, rather than that the client-worker relationship is a means to the end of working with the individual through sympathy and understanding. Some workers feel it "good work" if they can lead the client on to speak of highly confidential and personal affairs, and they may be helped to see that they are listening to the client's story only because they are a representative of the agency. It is necessary to know why the client gave the worker the "confidential" material. Was it because the worker "led him on," because it flattered him to receive such confidences; was it the client's great need to talk about the situation; or was it an effort on the part of the client to gain "sympathy" and perhaps divert the worker from other areas? These things affect the problem of gauging just what material is confidential. The same type of information which may be "confidential" to one individual is repeatedly discussed by another individual without conflict. When records are likely to be available to a number of non-professional people, it is necessary to use restraint both in content and style. Workers should distinguish between material which, though unpleasant or painful, is relevant to the problem and material which is irrelevant. The former belongs in the record; the latter probably not.

To repeat, there is no such thing as a model or pattern record, and in the professional record skill in practice and skill in recording are so closely interdependent as to be almost indistinguishable. Style will be conditioned throughout by the case-work concepts and practices reported. The best records contain not only objective facts, events, and behavior but are purposed to bring out clearly diagnostic thinking and treatment as well. Records may be short or long, but their constant use makes readability the most important single factor. The interest value or readability of a professional record derives directly and solely from the nature of the problems and the treatment, not from their picturesqueness or drama. The style, then, that brings out significant elements in situation and problem for treatment purposes most economically, accurately, and lucidly is inevitably good style. Records used for teaching and study purposes will tend to include more details of material being studied than do records used chiefly for practice. The ordinary rules of good English apply to the making of records readable, although symbols, abbreviations, and technical terms are permissible when the procedures indicated are in familiar professional use. Both the summary and recording-of-process methods of recording are good usage for appropriate material. Topical arrangement assists readability for certain kinds of subject matter; indexing assists readability in the chronological record. Diagnostic emphasis is fundamental, but the forms of it are extremely varied. Restraint and selection are always important, not only for the immediate purpose of brevity, but for the reason that in many agencies access to records is not sufficiently guarded.

VIII

SPECIAL PROBLEMS IN RECORDING

ALTHOUGH all fields confront much the same problems in recording—the social case record, like case work itself, being more generic than specific—administrative and functional considerations in agencies do pose certain questions for us. There is the problem in departmentalized agencies of the "unit" record; the problem of cross reference in agencies using the "patient" rather than the "family" record; the emphasis on intake material; what one might describe as the problem of the short record and the problem of the scientific and academic record, to mention only a few of the possible topics for discussion.

THE UNIT RECORD

All departmentalized agencies face the question of the unification of the total record. The so-called "mural" agencies, such as the court or the hospital, have to combine two or more different professional approaches, for example, legal-social or medical-social approaches. Other agencies have departmentalized bureaus within their framework (visiting nursing, visiting housekeeping, home economics, business- or vocational-guidance services) , the records of which must be combined. If the departments are physically inaccessible, so that each must keep a complete record, it seems to be more satisfactory to exchange carbons at intervals than to prepare summaries which are never ready when the department wants them. But this amounts to the duplication of records, which is always somewhat unsatisfactory. If departments preserve their identities to this extent, we have an "assembled" and not precisely a "unit" record. If the departments are physically accessible, the entries of a visiting housekeeper or consultant may be interspersed chronologically between the entries of the case workers or others. Many child-placing records which at first glance appear departmentalized are textually integrated. On the whole it is better to construct a unit record with the necessary library facilities for circulation among the departments concerned.

In medical-social work, the unit record is contributed to by physicians, social workers, nurses, and technicians. Administrative details of finance, bills, and so forth, are usually separated and kept in the superintendent's office or other appropriate place. The chart is concentrated on the treatment of the patient. Many social service departments still keep the social chart separately, putting only summarized material in the medical record, but the trend which has been strongly moving toward better medical-social integration finds its expression in a unit record. Sometimes each department (medical, nursing, social service) does its work-up on sheets of different colors and then shares a common follow-up page, entries succeeding each other chronologically, irrespective of whether they are medical or social notes. Because the social area is so complex, workers using the unit medical record have to subject themselves to rigid disciplines of selection and condensation lest the social material overwhelm

the medical. Many doctors, accustomed to medical ab-
breviation and hieroglyphics, will not take the time to
examine long social work entries, and even if they
would, the problem of bulk makes such documents
questionable. Social entries should be relevant, non-
technical and concise.

Objections to the unit record include the danger
that in large institutions the confidential nature of the
record may not be guaranteed. Even if records are not
subpoenaed, it is hard to protect intimate social material against casual examination. On the other hand,
unless library facilities are extremely accessible and
competently directed, the unit record may not be available to the several persons wanting simultaneous use
of it. A few agencies with departmentalized structure—
although this is not characteristic of medical work especially—prefer an assembled rather than a unit record.
Departmental notes are clipped or bound together and
inserted in a common folder or envelope to be withdrawn separately at will. This makes for greater flexi-
bility in the handling of records but defeats the unified
purpose, since departments tend to draw out only their
own special material.

Because so much medical-social treatment deals with
sick people, for whom management, mobilizing of resources, and so on, may be of an active type, or because
treatment may consist of interpretation of the medical
problem to patients and their families along the lines
indicated by the medical-social configuration, process
has to date not been much featured in the medical
record. Again we have in the relationship so delicate an
interplay among physician, worker, and patient that
the recording of worker-patient relationships *per se* has

not usually been stressed. The medical-social record has, until recently, featured services and environmental adjustments as over against behavior and relationship data of the sort familiar in child guidance, family work, and children's work. When direct interactive treatment, however, between client and worker does take place, it is important to indicate it. A supplementary record may be kept for self-study and other purposes. Most medical-social workers agree that it would be desirable to indicate more of the emotional factors in the patient's behavior and life situation, but the problem is no more manageable here than in other types of records, and the need for relevance, appropriateness, and conciseness is especially insistent in the unit record. Summaries are in places necessitated because of the orchestration, but for the most part very brief running entries pared down to essentials with a good deal of medical-social interpretation are characteristic.

Court records, like unit records in a hospital, are affected by the use made of the social material by another profession. The judge, perhaps even more than the physician, has by prestige the directing rôle in the case, and his time schedule, point of view, and legal tradition shape the presentation of data. The record mechanically and textually, through formal printed outlines, readily available summaries, and other structural devices, reflects the demand for quick reference. The kind of material gathered and presented has also been conditioned by legal attitudes as to what constitutes evidence and in probation by certain established procedures of supervision. It is hard to generalize here because in some courts the integration is around a distinctly legal focus and in others there is latitude for social work-up, interpretation, and after care, so that the resulting case record is like another case record in the behavior field except in the degree of formality with which authoritative legal opinion is stated.

The movement in probation has been steadily toward generic case work, with less insistence on legal evidence and court procedures.[1] Diagnostic material and comment by the probation officer are now encouraged by many judges; more emotional material is desired, and a less formal terminology is acceptable. Nevertheless, the defined periods of investigation, parole, rehearings, and so on, with a corresponding necessity for periodic analysis and reports in duplicate or triplicate, may give a distinct pattern to the case record. Consolidated reports, blocked and arranged topically, are more characteristic than chronological work-up, and even reports from other agencies may be presented within the consolidated work-up. Integration on the whole is achieved through binding and sequence, the departmentalized effect still dominating.

In child guidance clinics the unit record is found in its most integrated form. Although the psychiatrist, as in the case of the physician or judge, is the chief, each of the several studies—medical, psychological, social and psychiatric—has its own place of work-up, sometimes on sheets of different colors, and the findings are integrated and interpreted in a joint staff conference, which is usually reported in full. Integration is further achieved thereafter through shared staff conference minutes of diagnostic discussion and treatment evaluation, and also through interspersed chronolog-

[1] Some of the early judges like the early psychiatrists insisted that social studies be prepared without either social interpretation or recommendations, but fortunately more participating methods are becoming acceptable.

ical notes. If a psychiatrist is carrying a child through a series of treatment interviews, and a social worker is doing likewise for another patient in the group, each may continue to use separate sheets within the same folder. This creates a parallel record which has all the difficulties of separate sibling records in child placing; but perhaps this cannot be avoided. If there is only one major patient series, the environmental handling of the rest of the family group is subordinated and included in the single treatment narrative.

The Patient versus the Family Focus

Case work practice is traditionally family centered. The family field has used a single chart no matter how many persons were involved. Volume I is succeeded by Volumes II and III, and not by charts; i.e., John Smith, James Smith, and Helen Smith. Medical-social unit records, on the other hand, start from a patient focus, depending on which members of the family are undergoing medical treatment, and carry John, James, and Helen Smith on separate charts only when they become medical patients. One of these records may be selected to carry the master history, or carbons from other charts may be introduced, but it is more common to write short cross-reference notes than to carry carbon sets. Medical-social records which are not of the unit type generally carry all members of the family in a single family record. Each patient's situation will be focused, however, through devices of indexing and arrangement. Court and probation records have always a designated patient focus, and if more than one member of the family is a delinquent, a separate chart will usually be made for each.

In child guidance work the siblings in a family group, if patients at the clinic, will probably have separate charts, although the child and adult family records are not separated. In certain clinics and in some agencies in which a psychiatrist may have the child patient and a social worker the mother or father, or *vice versa*, or if two social workers are involved with different patients, both courses of treatment may appear on the same chart but running sequentially on sheets of different colors.

In the children's field the problem of cross reference is extremely difficult. If several siblings are placed out in different foster homes, the cross-reference complexity increases. A recent record, 1933, has in Section I a family part which contains referral situation, description of child and family at home, physical and psychological examinations of the child, family history and the account of the placing, follow-up on the child's own family, child's return home, and follow-up there. The dates cover the period March to July. Then there is an independent section, under the child's name, of a series of treatment interviews with the psychiatrist, March to December. Then a section, also under the child's name, of the direct contacts with the child by the worker, covering visits, trips to doctors' offices, placement of child, follow-up on foster home, emphasis on school, clothing, behavior of child and foster parents, continued psychiatric and health appointments, and so on. The period covered is March to July, when the child is returned home. In the first, or family, part the entry of 7/29/33 reads: "For details regarding Louisa's return home and visitor's conference with father and aunt, see child's record this date." The four or five pages ensuing deal with the child in the family in the child's section. Cross references in the family section are used. "4/8/33: For details regarding foster mother's impression of aunt, see child's record this date." "4/29/33: For details regarding report of father's interview at clinic, see child's record this date." One sees how complex is the recording problem here.

An investigation of a foster home, like other social study, is too long to reproduce, but a piece taken from a long report may be interesting. An analysis of the home follows nine pages of home visits, and reference calls, with such headings as "Mrs. G's Application," "Directions for Reaching Home," "Neighborhood," "Mr. G's Early Life," "Finances," "Experience with Children." The home is later evaluated in terms of the child's progress.

ANALYSIS OF FOSTER HOME

7/5/32.—The G's are an intelligent, middle-class couple with a genuine love for children and with experiences in their lives which have given them a finer and gentler attitude towards people rather than a critical one. Mr. G's rejection by his father and disappointment in his first marriage seem to have been offset by his feeling of success in his work and by the security he got from the relationship with his mother and now has in his marriage and by the acceptance of him by his wife's family. Mrs. G's experiences have been constructive for her, and her quiet forcefulness and understanding have no doubt brought out the best in Mr. G's character, while his generosity and admiration for her have given her much satisfaction. Their disappointment in not having children and Mrs. G's less active life since marriage have led to some loneliness, and it is apparent that they both need more interests. Their first happy experience in boarding attractive children may make it more difficult for them to accept a less responsive child, but the appeal of a child's need for them will be strong. Visitor feels they are discreet enough people to be trusted with full interpretation of parents' behavior and the causes, and that they will be tolerant. We felt on the whole that Mr. G was less mature and would need more praise and encouragement in supervision than Mrs. G.

While Mrs. G has a great need for a child, visitor does not believe that she will be possessive or fail to give a child normal outlets. There is a quietness about her and a knowledge of health care which would be good for a nervous child; one starved for affection would have both a father's and a mother's in this home. They prefer one or two boys or girls from two years up. The physical surroundings are good, though there is not much open space for active sports. There are not many children in the block, but Grace and Charles Sidney made friends and spent much time in play.

This home is recommended for one or two boys or girls from two to twelve years old. It would be best to place a fairly attractive and responsive child here, as the G's still have such a strong feeling for children they had and who were attractive, that there may be comparison or disappointment.

SIX-MONTH EVALUATION OF FOSTER HOME

1/15/33.—Sue Blank, born 4/5/23, was placed with Mr. and Mrs. G, whose home had been checked already on 7/5/32. She was a reserved and inhibited New England child who seemed too serious and old for her years. Her mother had been sent to a state hospital for the insane when she was 7 years old and Sue had been taken by a strict and narrow paternal aunt, in whose home the child lived for two years. Father disliked this aunt, and she disapproved of him. To have Sue near him he brought her to New York City.

Mr. and Mrs. G took Sue wholly and completely into the heart of their family life. They have shown a real interest and love for her without overdoing it. Sue responded quickly, and in the past eight months has blossomed out into a lively, normal little girl. She has made many friends and become popular at school, where her record for both work and behavior has been excellent.

Both Mr. and Mrs. G have made Sue feel their interest in her activities. They helped her fix up her room, encouraged her with other children, and gave her the puppies as her special charge. Mrs. G has shown insight and understanding in answering Sue's questions about her mother and father, about sex and the meaning of mental illness. Sue has turned to her with complete trust and confidence.

Mrs. G has received Mr. Blank in a friendly manner. Mr. G, however, understands him better and has helped to give Mrs. G a more tolerant and humorous attitude toward his shortcomings. Both Mr. Blank and Mr. G have had similar seafaring backgrounds. Mr. Blank is an immature individual, who as soon as his foot leaves shipboard likes to get drunk (though not overbearingly so) and have lady friends. It has been difficult to work out his desires with Sue's needs. Both Mr. and Mrs. G have shown a remarkable capacity for receiving and accepting our interpretations of father, without condemning him or developing too great a need to protect Sue from him.

We feel more sure of the good relationship between Mr. and Mrs. G. He is less mature in that he is more easily upset than she. On the other hand, he holds no grudges, and his hearty humorous manner has gone a long way in putting Mr. Blank at his ease. Mrs. G quietly manages Mr. G.

We have felt that she always remembers the unhappiness of his first marriage and wants to do all she can to make him happy now. She enjoys him, and when he gets "cocky" as he did at the time of our first worker's contact and says *"he"* is going to do this and that, Mrs. G laughs good-naturedly and comes back with some remark which shows she loves him and understands his need to feel himself an important man.

Sue has shown fondness and liking for him. Although he has not mentioned it to us directly, Mrs. G has told us that Mr. G has been taking night courses in engineering. He has had his salary cut, but not to a great degree. His health has been good. His face occasionally twitches, but this is covered by the heartiness of his manner.

Sue has gained 10 pounds since going to this home. She looks happy and robust now, and there is less tension and seriousness in her manner. Both Mr. and Mrs. G have responded well to supervision and, we feel, have gained much security from their relationship with the agency.

The children's field, like other fields, tended in the twenties to a structuralized record with summarized social study, the diagnostic work, medical, psychological and social, being concentrated while the child was in hand, so to speak, before placing, but the treatment remained usually chronological. Because of intake practices which obtain in family-children and children-and-court agencies in certain localities, it is still not unusual to find a child welfare record beginning with a summarized report of the antecedent handling; but the children's agencies which do a whole case work job, including intake, which think of the family as a unit and treat it in relation to the placed-out child or children, reveal this tendency in a family-unit type of record. The segmental record of the early children's field, like the departmentalized record of other agencies, seems to be passing, or at least to be greatly modified by integrative practices. Occasionally one sees an arrangement in which the family of origin has one folder, the foster family with placed-out children has a second folder of the family agency type, and each child has in addition his own folder; but in so far as the agency emphasizes work with the child's own family, as well as with the foster family, the more inclusive record will probably be undertaken. In all events the record will be designed by indexing, headings, colored pages, and other devices to bring out each child as patient within the family framework.

A reason occasionally given for the patient rather than the family record is that it is an administrative convenience in certain public departments, the collection of board and the billing of parents or state bureaus being on a per capita basis; but this can be achieved by separate forms within the record. Except in case of adoption or permanent placement the family unit record with treatment interwoven between own home and placed-out siblings is preferable when it can be managed. There will always be especially complicated child-placing situations for which neither the ordinary unit record nor the family record is practicable, and a series of cross-indexed folders must be utilized.

THE SHORT RECORD

The best way to shorten a record is to leave out everything which is not significant for immediate treatment purposes. The next best way to shorten a record is to cultivate a lucid, brief style, avoiding repetition and all padding whatsoever. Since this counsel of perfection calls for diagnostic expertness and good writing, we shall not labor the point. What most people mean by a short record is one of incidental service, that is, for cases which from the outset look immediate, simple, and likely to result in early closing out or referring. The question is, shall we write these records as if they were likely to be reopened or dispose of them as simply as possible? Writers who have habituated themselves to the recording of process have to make a distinct effort to adopt short-cuts, whether within long records or in writing incidental service records.[2] At the time of dictation one may be hazy as to the probability of reopening. However, when one is not hazy, when at the time of dictation the case is relatively complete, selectivity and restraint should be urged for the same reason that the closing entry should not usually be elaborated. The situation can be briefly indicated and

[2] An incidental service case is one really of minor study, an office type of inquiry being substituted for the more extended social study, the service undertaken being of the immediate and usually practical sort.

the action taken by the worker equally briefly indicated. The reason for closing or for referring, however,
should be quite carefully stated. The major problem
may be named rather than set forth in a diagnostic
statement, and even the expense of a folder and face
sheet may be obviated, although filing becomes then
more difficult. The record should, however, be on
paper of regular size so that if the case should be reopened it may be bound and started again in a formal
way if more intensive treatment is proposed.

Writers who never write long records will perhaps
see little sense in the above statement. They want to
know what goes into a short record and are impatient
with any sort of careful document. It is our observation
that the only discipline which permits one to write a
good short record is that which has taught one how to
write a good full one. Short records are legitimate in
any field, although writing a short record calls for very
clear thinking. All records could be improved by a developed sense of relevance and appropriateness of material.

A version of the short-record question was presented
by emergency relief agencies. This was not the question
of an "incidental service" type of record, however, but
of how brief one could be under pressure. A real problem in the mass relief field has been the notion that
records must be hastily and badly done. That disaster
relief records should be scarcely more than registration and action taken is inevitable; that mass emergency relief records should have little more than registration, eligibility procedure, and relief accounting is
natural. But once the relief agency settles down to
functional activity in public welfare, the recording

problem is generic. Certain questions about recording in relief administration are nevertheless expanded in the next chapter.

THE INTAKE PROCESS

Early case work procedures, at least in the family field, entrusted the first contact to a clerk or office secretary, who took down both registration data and the main features of the situation. The worker then made a visit at the home and obtained there, partly through question and answer and partly through friendly conversation, a full factual statement of present and past circumstances, which was later organized in the record into the so-called "first interview" of *Social Diagnosis*.[3] Some agencies still proceed in this way.

It is now considered better to have intake interviews conducted by professional persons, who may or may not be responsible for registration also. Registration is usually handled by a clerk, who also clears the case with the social service exchange. Intake interviews may be taken at the home, although the present tendency is to handle applications within the office.[4] Hospital admitting varies (among other factors) according to the responsibility for admission, that is, whether it is one hundred percent social service admitting or whether intake is shared by medical and administrative personnel and only a small fraction of cases seen by social

[3] Richmond, Mary, *Social Diagnosis*, Russell Sage Foundation, 1917.

[4] No arbitrary line can be drawn between one phase of intake and another. Theories articulated about admitting include allowing client to describe his need in his own way; assisting him to clarify the outline of his situation; explaining the purpose of the agency; estimating his capacity for handling his problem; preparing him for further activity, interviews or investigation at his home and so on. These intake phases may be divided differently among workers and the recording will inevitably be conditioned by the division of labor.

workers. It has been recognized that the person's immediate social situation, his attitudes toward hospitalization or relief, his resources, and his plans for himself are important, and this recognition is shown by the use of a much less historical introductory statement than was characteristic of earlier records.

The following illustrations are cited, not because they differ markedly from practices already described, but to show the client's own story at intake with some adaptation here of the recording of process, which may not be feasible for extensive use in the main body of a relief record. The danger is that of length.

INTAKE INTERVIEW A

Mrs. K made first application for relief. The family consists of Mr. K, born 1-28-1880 in N.Y.C., and Mrs. K, born 4-3-1880 in Germany. Also living in the same apartment are their daughter Jane, born 8-11-'05 in New York City, and her husband. They are Protestants.

Mrs. K makes a good appearance and presented her situation clearly and concisely, although she is considerably disturbed over what to do at the present time. She is aggressive, although pleasant in manner, and seems intelligent.

Mrs. K said that the first thing she wanted us to know was that her husband has been sick for the past year and a half. He had had two operations at Mercy Hospital, the first in July, 1933, when he had a ruptured appendix. He was in the hospital for 5 months at the time. He got pneumonia and because he was in the oxygen tank they could not perform the operation soon enough. He was left in such a weak physical condition that he had to have another operation in November, 1934, for abdominal rupture. He was in the hospital 4 weeks and was sent to Sea Breeze to convalesce. Therefore he has been home only a short time. The doctors told him to be careful and not to go back to his trade, which is that of silversmith, as it is too heavy. There is danger of his ripping out the stitches; there are both internal and external stitches. Her husband has been unable to find any lighter work, and that is why they have got so far behind in their rent. They owe 6 or 7 months now. Mrs. K would like some help to pay their back rent so they would not have to be put out of the house.

In response to our question as to how she has been getting along, Mrs. K said that her daughter is employed and pays board and room for herself and her husband. The husband is unemployed so the daughter is the only one who is working. It is impossible to pay the rent, which is $25 per month for 5 rooms, although Mrs. K tries to cut down on their other expenses as much as possible. Her fuel bill is $2.50 a week for coal, wood, and one piece of ice. She pays 50¢ a week on her husband's insurance which is the only insurance they have, and pays gas and electric, which leaves less than $3 a week per person for food. Her daughter earns $20 a week as a clerk and pays $15 a week to her parents. The remaining $5 she uses for her own carfare and lunches and expenses. Mrs. K says they have exhausted all other resources, as she cashed in the other insurance they had had.

The amount of income is in excess of home relief budget even if only $15 a week is counted as income. This would be $65 a month, and even if the full rent of $25 were paid, there would be a balance of $40 a month for other expenses. Budget for food, household, gas, and electricity comes to $32.15 monthly. We explained this to Mrs. K.

Mrs. K said that she did not know what to do; she guessed that the only thing for her was to break up her home. As she seemed quite disturbed, we told her that there were agencies in the community that she could try, if she wished, although we did not know whether they would be able to help her either. We gave her the address of the Bay District of the Family Society.

Status of case: application rejected.

The first illustration in as-it-happened style, is somewhat condensed, but in illustrations "B" and "C," which are too long to cite, the client's behavior and conversation are reproduced and process is indicated more fully.

INTAKE INTERVIEW B

Excerpt

When Mr. S returned to the interviewing room, he clenched his hands until the knuckles were white. He began repeating over and over that he would soon get work. Everything else is all right. They are bothering him about the rent, but he guesses they will wait. He got the gas turned on by asking for credit without the deposit. They said they would trust him for two weeks. They haven't any electricity. That is all right. They can burn candles. The baby has a cold. They are heating from the gas stove. They haven't much furniture. They lived in a furnished room before. They have a bed. It is a featherbed, so they can keep warm although they have no bedding. They really haven't any furniture except the stove and the bed, but that's all right. When he works they will get it. He will probably get work tonight. We wondered if Mr. S was trying to convince us or himself. Mr. S laughed nervously. He has got to get work. Things are a lot worse than you are really telling, aren't they, we said? Tears came to Mr. S's eyes. He got up and walked to the window. He has got to get work. Maybe he can tell us Monday that he has work. We wondered if they had any food at home. There is half a box of oatmeal. There is some tea. He is sure there's some sugar, that's all. Mr. S was given $2, and an immediate home visit was promised. He turned at the door to thank us and again said he hoped he was not imposing. He knew some people did.

INTAKE INTERVIEW C

Excerpt

We asked how they had managed lately, and he said that often when his wife went to City Hospital, Social Service would give her $1 for food. This is all they had. They are in arrears with the rent. He has a shut-off notice on the electricity. He just cannot remember anything. He feels like a baby breaking down under it all. He is falling to pieces. He does not think he could have gone on very much longer. He has come to the point now where he does not even know his own strength. His wife used to be fat; now you should see her. She used to weigh 169 lbs., but she is afraid to get on the scales now. "I haven't slept for weeks; and yet I feel so tired it seems to me I could sleep on tacks, but when I go to bed there is no rest for me, no sleep of any kind." He continued: "No, Miss, this hanging around is bad, this getting pushed around with no satisfaction; it has been terrible." Again he repeated that this was the first kindness he had had in months. Somehow this kind of business can make a fellow steal. He paused. We said, "You fear that this will happen to you." He looked up and with a serious expression on his face, said "That's what I've always been afraid of. It wouldn't be anything to me, but my God, my wife—what would happen to her if I went to prison. It's only her I think about. It's been her that's been worrying me these months. My family is mad at me because I married her. They did not like her, and I haven't seen any of them." We wondered which aunt it was with whom he had been living, and he told us that it was his father's sister. She was the only one that was nice to him, but she was poor herself and on home relief. They are an old couple, and his uncle was very sick. They were janitors when he lived with them. He just doesn't know how they have kept along. They have had no decent food for weeks. . . .

The main point of emphasis is that intake interviewing has shifted from a complete factual first interview to the considerations: What is the client suffering from; what does the situation look like; what has he done or can he do about it himself? What does he want us to do? Is it within our function to help him and if so what are the next steps to take together. In recording, this type of interview is reflected less well by a topically arranged summary than by a running as-it-happened arrangement.

Additional examples of intake interviews in public welfare will be found in the succeeding chapter.

RESEARCH AND TEACHING

Our discussion thus far has approached the record from the point of view of value in practice. Social workers keep records because they are thereby assisted in thinking in a less fragmentary way about the clients' problems. That for scientific appraisal these records are incomplete, inaccurate, and subjective is undoubtedly true. Even for practice, records may be stereotyped or biased. Laboratory tests of accuracy in recall will always show so high a percentage of errors as to suggest that incidents or interviews reported after the event are not dependable. Several factors, however, do operate to make the record in skilled hands a tool, if not of precision, then of pragmatic value.

The habit of note taking has gained ground. At one time even face-card information was a *tour de force* of memory; now registration is recorded in a direct business-like way. In some cases blanks or forms are used; in others, interviews by competent persons. Moreover, the increased use of office interviewing permits longer case notes to be made, sometimes during the interview, if the content is informational and without emotional significance for the client, sometimes immediately after the interview. Note taking during or after home visits has always been much less practicable. Other factors which may be conducive to accuracy are the habit of reporting observed behavior in verbal rather than adjectival terms and of quoting directly phrases used by the client.

Another check is the repeated impact of sequential interviews, all carefully recorded. There is no substitute for the kind of accuracy which comes from giving one's undivided attention to approximately the same phenomena in a restricted field of vision over long periods of time. The fact that clients tend to bring up the same conflicts increases the reliability of repeated observations. The introduction of masses of data does not make a document more scientific. It is the accuracy of the observation and the disciplined and experienced sense of significance which tend to make records more scientific.

Increased training in diagnostic statement sharpens the problem sense, and as the treatment has grown more conscious and purposive one is more able to estimate drifts and interconnections. How valuable the ordinary practice record is for research is not altogether clear. Most people agree that the ex post facto use of records to throw light on arbitrarily selected questions has very limited possibilities. A somewhat naïve hope persists that by taking a few hundred records light will be thrown on the working of a compensation law or the effect of relief on family life or on housing conditions. In order that records may be useful in this way, the problem must be selected in advance, and special types of inquiry must be instituted if the data are to be available in specific, concrete form. Records so built up have a contribution which run-of-the-mine records cannot yield.

Yet even our still too-haphazard records do supply, in what is popularly called "face-card information," certain units such as family composition, wages, marital status, nationality, and the like which can be counted. Such data may be computed routinely from most records and are the basis of many reports. Other units of case accounting taken directly or indirectly from records may include the number of open and closed cases, analysis of applications, amounts of board paid, relief spent, number of children given boarding care, and so on.[5] These are administrative "production" items. More difficult items to classify are those concerned in the naming and indexing of social problems. Case workers as a rule prefer definition, as in the diagnostic statement, to classification, and the agreement here that classification is not a useful tool unless the relationships of the items to be classified are quite fully known is probably correct. The nature of social interaction and the fact that the social case is not an aggregation of units but a configuration with a meaning does make its analysis into factors and the classification thereof peculiarly unsatisfying. Moreover, the case worker's "emotional attachment"[6] to the "human elements of a case," to quote Professor George Lundberg, is part of this sense of wholeness and may not be altogether an error.

The case worker's attachment to the human element is indeed real, and for him all social phenomena offer important emotional constituents. To indicate these emotional constituents is one of the hardest problems in recording and one of the items least susceptible to counting. The current attempt to reproduce the living organism in behavior through the recording of process is motivated in large part by the hope that through intensive observation and treatment, through even a single relationship, emotional problems can be revealed and in some measure worked out. That technique and data here are far too insubstantial as yet to be reduced

[5] Fisk, Helen I., *Statistical Recording and Reporting in Family Welfare Agencies,* Family Welfare Association of America, 1934.

[6] For a full discussion of case studies and the statistical method, see Lundberg, George A., *Social Research,* Longmans, Green, 1929, p. 180, in which he supports the position that the statistical method furnishes the only means "whereby the individual case becomes at all comprehensible or scientifically significant."

to schedules does not mean that schedules and outlines may not sometime be employed to clarify the picture too often haphazardly drawn.

Experts in social research differ with regard to the value they attach to direct study and penetration. On the one hand, Professor Waller states that if one perceives a single instance correctly he can generalize from that instance.[7] On the other hand, the classical research position stresses the point that empirical generalization is extremely dangerous and that statistical method is the soundest tool in formulating abstract concepts. Probably agreement would be general that experimentation out of "pre-existing insights" is better than shotgun types of inquiry and that one must caution oneself to quantify only such material as can be realistically counted.

A careful use of everyday words and a greater number of technical terms and phrases precisely defined will help us in the comparing and tabulation of items.

Today the use of social case records is probably more extensive for teaching purposes than for research. The classroom teacher of social case work relies on a series of life situations to illustrate typical processes. The wise teacher does not create a syllabus and then try to find perfect illustrations for it but selects case situations intrinsically sound and develops the syllabus around it. Range is assured by choosing cases from different fields of practice and with different problem emphases. For technical emphases bits of case material, single interviews, or incidents are common. Procedures like those of intake, child-placing, and relief-giving can be illus-

[7] Waller, Willard, *Insight and Scientific Method, American Journal of Sociology*, Vol. XI, November, 1934.

trated with parts of case records even when the detailed technical elements are obscure or not otherwise satisfactory.

Case records used by students in the field tend to be over-elaborated for supervisory purposes. One can rarely observe students in action during the interviewing process, and teachers, therefore, try to get full details expressed which may show how the student has proceeded. When he is taught from the beginning to put in everything, because as yet for him relative significance is unknown, he may tend to redundancy long after his diagnostic sense has sharpened. Students trained from the beginning to summarize and analyze may show the opposite defect of not being able to report a significant incident accurately and patiently. If all students could have training in social history summaries as well as in the more or less verbatim reporting of interviews and then could be trained in analyses in which everything must be sharpened and condensed, we should have records more satisfactory alike for observed data and for problem sense. As it is now, student records are apt to swing from an elaboration of the obvious to a formal rigidity of outline which is equally unreadable.

Staff workers also are tempted to lengthen records either for self-supervisory conferences or for supervisory inspection. In general the tendency is to overwrite the processes we are least familiar with. When social workers were learning how to investigate the social circumstances of an applicant, every step was given. When certain elements in social inquiry became habitual, records then began to carry blocked and arranged studies with source material indicated. When interpretation was first undertaken, diagnostic summaries were a scheme of categories. The much simpler diagnostic statement of today shows greater ease with the same material. Another reason for detail in records is rapid turnover. Before the worker can catch the drift of the case or weigh the relationships adequately, he is gone, and another worker must examine the evidence. In agencies with low turnover and without students, marked condensation usually appears, although here the temptation to carry the case too long in the head and too little on the dictaphone may be the danger.

The time cost of a case record is said to be about two dollars a page at present salary averages, so that again we must balance the uses of the record for practice, teaching, and research, and try to make differentiated use of this important tool. We certainly should not write all records with a research schedule in mind, nor should we evade the responsibility of careful description of what appears to be important in order fully to explore a problem.

To summarize: in departmentalized agencies the unit record appears to be gaining ground, although it is still apt to be assembled in one folder rather than integrated. Balance and orchestration are desirable. In hospitals and courts the medical-social and legal-social elements must be focused. The specialties should not be isolated but integrated in a main social-case-work theme. In so far as the patient rather than the family unit is stressed, some parallel recording may take place with the use of separate charts or separately arranged pages within the chart. The recording of staff diagnostic and treatment conferences are integrative devices, and when it is convenient to use a common follow-up page for treatment, this too has advantages. The fewer cross references one's system requires, the better for all concerned.

In all fields intake interviews are now quite carefully reported. Workers following the fashion of recording process should be cautioned against overextending material in the record either with direct quotation or other data if the applicant's handling of the interview is meager, trivial, or insignificant. Conversation and behavior are not necessarily revealing, and the old rule is still sound—in case work do not neglect the obvious, but in recording do not labor it.

Records developed for active practice should, on the whole, be held to clarity, brevity, and diagnostic insistence, with only enough data to particularize the problem-treatment themes. Records in limited quantities may be developed much more fully to describe people's behavior and accounts of themselves for experimentation, for special studies, or in order to help train students.

That case records focused to single social situations provide little material for the exploration of larger social issues is also a limitation, since we have not yet devised satisfactory ways of indexing these type situations. The index of social problems kept by social agencies is still casual and superficial. The pendulum has been swinging so far away from indexing and classification that we may expect fresh attempts in this direction before long. At present the preoccupation in all fields is to find some satisfactory ways of recording human relationships in their more dynamic aspects.

IX

RECORDING IN PUBLIC ASSISTANCE

BECAUSE of the rapid expansion in public assistance agencies during the last few years, it may be timely to devote a chapter to special problems in this one field. Public welfare records are of the family agency type and follow in the main the practices described elsewhere. It is important to remember that just as in a medical-social record the medical features of the case should be clearly denoted, so in relief administration the economic or financial-social data should be central. The two main aspects of the recording lie in practices incident to eligibility, to budget, and other more or less standardized procedures, and in practices incident to the treatment of the client's[1] behavior, attitudes, or family problems in his unique relief situation.

Workers are not always interested in or careful about the recording and revision of budgets, largely because of lack of training. And if, as in some places, workers are not themselves responsible for requisitioning or handling the grants, they will need additional instruction in order to accent, both in their case work and the recording, the appropriate emphasis. On the other hand, because of the perennial interest of the public

[1] The terminology in this field is still far from satisfactory. Recipients of aid are called "clients," "grantees," "allottees," and so forth, and the income referred to as "grants" or "allowances" in the social security categories and "relief" in general public assistance. For most case-record purposes the client's own name or initial—"Mr." or "Mrs. H."—seems simplest, with "applicant" or "client" used when relevant.

in direct relief expenditure, there is always a tendency to take too much of the worker's time and too much record space in duplicate relief bookkeeping. The more details of financial transactions of the cashier kind of activity that can be kept out of the case record, the better. The bookkeeping must be accurately done, but it should not be done in the case record. The professional worker is responsible for describing the family finances, for estimating and recording the family budget, for periodic comments on the rate and nature of the relief, and particularly for noticing any changes. But the actual posting of grocery orders, money payments, and so on is a clerical accounting job which should be dealt with through ledgers and other devices. Workers should know the curve in the relief, however, and may keep rough totals of the amount granted, may consult the ledger card from time to time, or better still may be furnished periodically by the accounting department with totals drawn from the ledger. These totals may then appear on a card, in the text, or in periodic summaries.

A question usually arises in connection with forms. Public records tend to the use of forms because of the necessity for standardization in accordance with governmental framework. Most agencies have the problem of duplicating forms, but the public relief agency is especially cumbered with overlapping data, among application blank, face sheet, budget card, and statistical card. Confronted by this array, many workers try to evade the issue by carrying these data around with them in their field books. Workers should be trained to relinquish the bulk of financial, identifying, and permanent data to the proper record forms and to keep their notebooks for more immediate observations. They should also read the records more and rely less on their own notes. It is important to have one good simple face sheet, although an application blank, if used, may be a practical substitute, and if it is administratively necessary to copy face-sheet material upon several cards, efficiency suggests that the arrangement and naming of the material on the several forms be similar. It is difficult to copy an item in an upper left-hand box on one form and have the same item appear, with a slight variation, in a lower right-hand box on another form.

The most frequent combination is that of face-sheet material on the front of an 8 x 11 card, and a budget on the back, ruled to permit revisions. This card belongs in the case record but may also be used as a desk file in an alphabetized box for each worker. There are advantages and disadvantages in having this card either in the case record or in a desk file. Obviously the chief point is that since it is and should be much used, this card should be accessible at all times, both with and without the rest of the record. Face-sheet material and detailed budget computation should not be repeated in the text; but changes in family status or of relief granted or other pertinent comment should appear in the text.

A recently evolved budget form features two stages of budget making—first, a basic eligibility type of computation; second, special needs to be figured as the circumstances require.

One controversial element has been introduced by the auditing problem.[2] Some auditors, both state and

[2] The auditor referred to here is the financial auditor associated with the comptroller's function. "Case reviewers" or "social auditors," that is, case workers assigned to this task from the Welfare Department, are qualified by experience to read and evaluate eligibility data.

BUDGET SHEET

Estimated Needs and Income	Date ☐1 Expires	Date ☐2 Expires	Date ☐3 Expires	Date ☐4 Expires	Date ☐5 Expires	Date ☐6 Expires
Monthly ☐						
Semimonthly ☐						

		1	2	3	4	5	6
Basic Needs	1 Shelter						
	2 Food						
	3 Fuel (cooking)						
	4 Fuel (heating)						
	5 Light						
	6 Incidentals or household supplies						
	7 Expenses of employment						
	8 Clothing						
	9 Medical supplies						
	10						
I	11 Total Basic Needs						
Income	12						
	13						
	14						
	15						
II	16 Total Income						
III	17 Basic Budget Deficit (I–II)						
Additional Needs	18 Carfare						
	19 Ice (summer only)						
	20 Heating (winter only)						
	21 Special diet						
	22						
	23						
	24						
IV	25 Total Addl. Needs						
V	26 Total Budget Deficit (III+IV)						
	Initials of investigator						

federal, start from the assumption that they must check the validity of the eligibility data through the case record. This would seem as inappropriate as by auditing hospital finance to supervise admission of patients. Obviously the determination and review of eligibility is a welfare, not an auditing function. It is proper that some summarized financial data report or card, with or without budget compilation, should be made available to auditors, but the case record is a study and service document, written not for fiscal or auditing purposes, but designed for everyday use by the persons most concerned and those most competent to shape it to efficient welfare practice.

The exacting regulations governing eligibility in the field carry an administrative counterpart in the office. Thus, in preparing the case record the report of eligibility must be carefully covered, with the appropriate recommendation; financial and social data cards must be figured and revised with notification as to changes in rate of grant. Orders connected with relief in kind, such as milk or clothing, must be checked, although not in the case record. Cases must be reviewed for reauthorization, and so forth. These appropriate and skilled operations are, however, often found overlaid with inappropriate clerical duties, thus making the necessary eligibility, budgetary, and authorization procedures irksome and protracted. Among inappropriate activities are found the writing of vouchers, filing and tracing records, mailing checks, posting grants, typing, and the like. On the other hand, financial data cards, monthly reports, case-load analyses, statistical counts, and authorization and reauthorization reports must be prepared as part of the administrative function. Sometimes the demands of a statistical department are excessive. It is part of the administrator's responsibility to see that statistical, accounting, and case procedures supplement and inform, but do not exploit, each other. In far too many organizations the notifications go from case to business, without a corresponding service from business to case; and the statistical department is all too frequently a one-way function. The effect of interchange and joint planning is almost always a reduction and simplification of forms. When services, such as resource departments and nutrition departments, become isolated, they not only tend to function extravagantly, but usually, to everyone's inconvenience, give birth to quantities of forms and reports and to what are virtually duplicate case records. Nevertheless, forms, indisputably useful, devised for processess specialized out of the inquiry into need include, besides budget forms, occupational sheets, insurance adjustment, mortgage and property blanks, and bank-clearing inquiries and medical data. Forms intended for the case record should be of approximately the same size and shape but may be differentiated by color. Forms intended for administrative purposes can be of any shape suitable for filing.

If it is important to reduce the total number of forms in the record, it is equally so to reduce the number of successive issues of the same form. If a new application blank is filed, it is not necessary to retain the old one. Any discrepancy or change should be noted on the new blank and referred to in the text. The old blanks may then be destroyed. The notion that restitution proceedings depend on the presence in the record of old application blanks seems to be neither true nor useful.

Old relief authorizations should not be retained. The date of approval of grant will appear on the financial- and social-data card. There is some reason to keep the last one or two relief authorizations, purely for the convenience of the social worker; but stacks of these, or of Social Service Exchange clearing slips, or of work-referral duplicates, do no one any good. Lists of voucher numbers are not appropriate in the case record, or procedures which have to do with the normal routing of complaint letters, or the like.

The public assistance record suffers from an excess of procedures as well as forms. Standardized procedures involving work referral or medical care, like those involving eligibility and authorization, call for orderly and accurate notation; but so far as possible, mechanics, as well as trivialities, should be avoided. A long list of phrases for probable omission would include "Worker compiled a budget as follows"; "Worker will notify Miss L of the result of the interview"; "Miss R called worker Friday afternoon requesting an appointment given for 3-2-36"; "Interview took about one half hour"; "Worker left interview to consult supervisor"; "Mr. Jones said that since he is not working he would call at the office the following day"; "A further report may be obtained after next Monday"; "2 quarts of milk approved by supervisor"; "Mr. D then left the department, thanking worker for his time"; "Took off wet coat at worker's suggestion"; "Received and read case"; "Sent new authorization to order-writing department"; "Checked February payroll. All three names are included, but the address has not been changed."

Entries concerning the making of appointments should be omitted unless there is something significant about the circumstances. When Mrs. R calls, it will be quite soon enough to comment, if comment is needed; and likewise with Mr. Jones who either will or won't call at the office on the following day. Usually the redundancy is accidental, occurring because the dictation period precedes the expected appointment. Routine relief issuance steps, routine follow-up letters, and the ordinary courtesies of the ordinary interview should also be omitted. Contrast with the above, the useful notations "Received a telephone message that Frank had been laid off at Wallace's—verified," or "Mollie at office having been sent for by worker because of reports about her reactions to information given her." It may be argued that procedural entries protect the worker; but the writer cannot agree, believing that regular weekly dictation periods of three to four hours' duration, supplemented by the use of appointment books, day sheets, notebooks and countersigned carbon copies of authorization forms are far better devices than a case record loaded with insignificant details. Long-hand notes for urgent attention may be resorted to, although they should be destroyed after the week's dictation period or as soon as attended to.

Agencies may fall into the bad habit of including in the transfer summary minute, procedural directions for the next relief authorization; for example

9-4-35: Family moving out of district.
Unit of 3—man, woman and 4 yr. old son.
Food allowance $10.60.
Rent allowance $8.70.
No gas and light allowance.
SC-4 completed.
Moving to new address, where light and gas allowance
   is needed 518 W. 213, Apt. 3C.
Regular visiting day Thursday, Buff.

The first two items will appear on application blank or face sheet—the first under the heading "New Address," the second under "Family Make Up." The following items will appear on the financial data card, which should be attached, and in a long-hand note attention may be called to the new gas and light arrangement. The completion of SC-4 (statistical card), after all, should be assumed, or in its incomplete form the card could be included in the folder; and the regular visiting time again should be mentioned in a long-hand note if there is no check mark on the financial data card. Concurrently the business office should transfer whatever fiscal cards should accompany the case record.

A procedure note like the following has, however, obvious validity:

9/13/36: Received notice that on 9/19 Smiths will receive check for $16.80. Not at home. Notice slipped under door.

Supervisory notes of a procedure sort have no place in the permanent record; for example:

10/1/36: Memo to Unit Supervisor from Case Supervisor, asking to have call made to see why client refuses to coöperate. If no valid reason, must close case ——

Supervisory conferences belong in the text, when they have the value of diagnostic or treatment-evaluation comment, but not when they reflect simple administrative controls.

As for the main style of the record, there are those who contend that in a public agency chronological entries are safer, since in the event of mistakes or complaints or appeals or special investigations they afford greater protection to client, worker, and administrator.

Supervisors with untrained staffs often encourage the chronological entry so that they can see the course of investigation and service more easily; but it is certainly true that in competent hands discrimination, selective summary, diagnostic work, and condensation of all kinds are not only economical but also adequate. Possibly in another decade or two, basic procedures will be so well understood and professional disciplines so thorough that symbols will be accepted. Then, no doubt, social work will be attacked not because the records are costly, as at present, but because some investigating politicians cannot read them!

The first requisite today is an effective clean-cut way of making visible the eligibility picture. Whether the workers should use the chronological form of entry, showing the step-by-step procedures for establishing eligibility or whether they should give a summarized report of the social study is decided by the operating agency. Certainly it is a convenience to have the eligibility data arranged and displayed in usable reports at intervals in the case record, from which a financial- and social-data card can readily be compiled. These data, especially in long-time allowance cases, need not be repeated; only changes need be noted and status reaffirmed or disavowed. If a topical report follows chronological entries already in the record, the summary will be briefer than if it carries the full report of the investigation without previous notes. In general public assistance as in other types, the client's own story at intake should be recorded more carefully than was common in the "emergency" agencies. A direct narrative style is usually preferable. It is not necessary to report the initial application interview verbatim or in full detail; but because it reveals the client's own sense of what is wrong, the story may well be given with selected use of the applicant's own phraseology, reflecting his own emotional stresses.[3]

The application blank has a standardizing and self-registration value and also the value of putting the responsibility on the client; the objection to it is that in the less professional agencies it is likely to be substituted for the client's own story at intake and so to start the record of Hamlet with Hamlet left out. The application blank is efficient, especially when combined with the appointment system, for the casual applicant who applies because "everybody else is stopping in." The following interview, although atypical in that the man had already been assigned to work relief (as has not infrequently happened), shows a good recording balance between factual material and the interviewing process, but it is unnecessarily long.

INTAKE INTERVIEW[4]

Moran, James.—M in office in response to letter to discuss his present family situation in order to determine his eligibil-

[3] Questions dealing with eligibility should also be included in the reported material with the appropriate topics indexed in the margin.

[4] A training district of a public agency, commenting on the recording of intake says: "We have found the most useful way to record the intake interview is the 'running record' form; that is recording the interview as it occurred, giving a brief statement at the beginning, setting the stage as it were, describing the attitude of the applicant and the family unit for whom relief is requested. For example, 'Mrs. B, a widow, applied for relief for herself and two children, John 19 and Mary 17. Her manner was frank and open and she talked freely throughout the interview but repeatedly referred to her embarrassment about having to apply for relief.'—Following such an introduction would come the client's statement of the situation and from there the mutual exchange of points brought up for discussion by both client and interviewer. We feel that this method of recording gives a clearer picture of the situation, because of the feeling tone included, than a topical outline which tends to standardize and de-individualize the content of the interview. Marginal headings used with the running record point up the material and are extremely useful

ity to continue on work relief. We explained to Mr. M that we had never been able to find him home and that an investigation into his financial circumstances is necessary if he is to continue on work relief. We explained further the eligibility requirements for work relief as being the same as those for home relief. M told us that he got the work relief job from the CWA at the State Employment office about one year ago. He earns $24 bi-weekly. He said that no one has ever been out to investigate him, although he has made out "thousands" of application blanks. There is no home relief application in the record.

Residence.—The family consists of man, woman and two children.[5] M said that they moved to the present address about 11-15-34. They have two rooms with steam heat at $20 a month, with their own furniture, and no private bath. They formerly lived, from July to Nov., 1934, at East —— St.; from April-July, 1934, at East —— St.; from December, 1933, to April, 1934, at East —— St. From March to December, 1933, M lived at —— St. Prior to this he lived at East —— St., Brooklyn. At one point in getting this information M said that he lived at East —— St. He had a good deal of difficulty remembering the addresses and dates of places he had lived and finally said that he had not lived at this place at all. He said he could not remember, as he had moved so much.

M has been married about three years and he has been in the United States about 7 years. M said he was born in England, but was raised in Ireland. W was born in Ireland, but came to the United States when she was nine years old.

Employment.—M is a master plasterer by trade. When he first came to this country, he worked for his uncle, Peter M, who is a contractor in Grand Rapids, Michigan. The name

in finding particular data in later reference to the interview. Emphasis needs to be put on economy in recording but not to the exclusion of all process which indicates the activity in the interview, that is, the interplay between client and interviewer. We do not need to include every 'worker asked—client replied,' but if the interviewer notices that the client seemed to block or shy away from discussion of some particular point, it is significant to record this for the future use of the visitor. The mechanics involved in the intake interview are completing the information on the registration card, and issuing an application blank to applicants eligible to apply."

[5] It is not necessary to repeat in the text the family composition, which appears on the face sheet as do also the residence data.

of his firm is M and Maloney. M used to earn $14 a day. He never belonged to a union. He has paid the full sum of his union membership to a man who turned out to be a fake and as he refused to pay this amount again he had to leave the job. He worked for his uncle from 1927 to 1929 and then came to the city. He has worked for the American Company on West Street as a baler, operating a machine at $27.50 a week. This was for one year, 1929-30. This was the only regular job he had in the city. He stated he was unemployed for over three years.

Bank account.—We asked M if he had any money saved at the time he left Grand Rapids and he said he had had $7,000 which he put into his uncle's bank. His uncle drew the money out and sent it to M. This was exhausted about two years ago, about a year before he got the work relief job. M's uncle lives on North Street, Grand Rapids, Michigan. M said that in the year before he got the work relief job, he did some odd jobs. One of these was at the New England Machine Company on West —— Street, repairing machines for about 3 months in 1933. M said that he is an all round worker.

Insurance and debts.—M said that he had one policy on himself in the New York Life Insurance Company which he surrendered for about $100 about 2 years ago. There is no insurance at the present time. M has no debts now. He has not had to borrow. When we asked if he had any current household debts, M said that he had had some before he got the work relief job, but that these are paid up. As he had no other work outside the work relief job we asked how he had managed to run his house and pay up his back debts on $12 a week. M said that he borrowed $300 from a friend named Bill Hal, who is living at present at East —— Street. M said that he had played the horses once and won over $400. His luck was so good that he has never played them since. He paid the $300 debt from this amount.

Relatives.—M's sister, Dorothy, lives in Auburn, New York. M's parents are dead, and he has no other relatives here. He did have a brother here, who died a few months ago. W's parents, John and Lucy Harrow, live in Ireland. W is an only child.

Discussion of relief policies.—M asked if we were trying to get jobs for the CWA people. We explained that we had only work relief jobs here and that these are given only to the people who are in need. That is the reason we have to make sure that people have no other resources and nothing to depend on except this job. He would like to be able to get off this job and added, jokingly, that he would give us a week's notice if he can. He said further that he does not think much of some of the men on this job. He had two years of college before he came to this country. He thinks you have to be smart to get along in this country. He thought when he came here that he was going to be laid off, so he got a note from his foreman, which stated: "Mr. M is a laborer for the CWA and one of the best men in a gang of 65, and as a worker he is everything I could ask for."

We told M that we did not think he would be laid off if this investigation were completed satisfactorily. We would like to have him make out an application blank and return it to us tomorrow with proof of his residence and the children's birth certificates. At this point M said explosively that he did not think that he cared about this job if he had to go through any more red tape. We discussed the necessity for "red tape." M did not know if his wife would sign the application blank. He talked of his feeling that home relief people are detectives. If he were laid off the job, he would not want to go on home relief, as he thinks "this is lower than normal." We stated that we realized it might be a blow to his independence. M thought he would like to get a job for himself rather than go through any more investigation. He asked for time to try to do this. We explained that it was necessary for us to have the application blank returned if he is to continue on the work relief job.

2/18/35.—M returned the application blank. He had written at the top of it that he lost both children's birth certificates. We noticed on the application blank that the children were listed as William, born 4/1/31, and Paul, born 10/15/32. When M came into the interviewing room he said immediately that his wife said she had lost the children's birth certificates. We asked M if he had really had these two children. M said, without embarrassment, that he did. We told M that we asked him the question because he had given quite different information about them on the application blank to

what he had told us yesterday. We told him what this discrepancy was and asked M if he remembered that he had told
us that his youngest child was "just a little baby" less than a
year old; and now, he writes down on the application blank
that the youngest child is over two years old. After a long
pause, M said: "Well, I guess you can't overlook it." We
agreed and asked him what the truth of the situation is. M
said that the truth is that he has no children at all. In response to our question M said that he feared that as interviewer had thought that he did have, he would be laid off the
job if he said he had no children. There was quite a long
discussion. He told us he would not take home relief even
though he would be laid off now. He feels that everybody is
entitled to a job and that it was smart of him to keep this one
as long as he did. He evidently feels no guilt about it, but is
also quite sincere in his desire to work.

There was further discussion of the economic and relief
situation in general. We asked M if he even had a wife. He
said, smilingly, that as long as he was telling the truth, he
might as well tell the whole truth. He did not have a wife
either. He got the job honestly enough in the beginning and
only invented the story about his family in order to keep it
when this investigation began . . .

Two home visits show topical and narrative weighting, respectively, suggested by the differing amounts of
factual as contrasted with behavior and attitude material.

HOME VISIT
Topical method

Neighborhood and Home.—Mr. and Mrs. T live at 68 Wil-
low Street in a front apartment on the second floor. It is a
part business and part residential section, filled with push-
carts and playing children. The family live in a modern
walk-up apartment house; steam heat and private bath are provided for each apartment. The apartment consists of four
rooms, and the rental is $31 per month. The furniture is of
good quality, but not new, and it shows evidence of better
days. The home was in good order and very clean.

Worker was received hospitably by Mr. T, who is a slender man of medium height. He appeared to be despondent and not in good health. He was pale, and worker felt that he showed an attitude of helplessness. Mr. T's clothes were worn shiny, but they were clean and pressed. Mrs. T's clothes were of good quality, and she seemed to expect much more of the Bureau than her husband and was very insistent that the Bureau should pay Wallace's carfare to school so that he may continue his studies. She also wanted clothes for the boys.

Attitude of Family.—Mr. and Mrs. T were entirely opposite in their attitudes toward the worker. Although both showed worker the greatest courtesy, Mr. T was quiet and despondent, telling how much he would appreciate anything that could be done for him. He did not seem to worry about himself so much, but he did want food for his wife and children. He told worker that he had always supplied them with a good home and plenty of food. He just could not see his wife and children hungry. He had no food in the house and threw ice-box doors open to substantiate his statement.

Residence.—Mr. T was not able to show any residence verification at this time, because he has only lived at present address for the last three months and all bills have been thrown away on the date of last moving. He was dispossessed from his former home. Mr. and Mrs. T are both American citizens, although they were both born in Poland. Mr. T came to U. S. A. at the age of 12 together with his father. He landed in Boston, and his first year was spent in school completing the first grade. The next year he worked for his uncle in a tailor shop. He completed another year of school by attending night classes. Mrs. T landed in N. Y. C. in 1904. She lived in N. Y. with her parents and completed a high school course.

Family.—After their marriage the couple settled in New York City. There are two boys in the family, Wallace and Max. Wallace is 15 years old; 6 feet, 4 inches tall, weighs about 165 lbs., and wears a size 14 shoe. He is unusually tall for his age; Mr. T stated that Wallace did not seem to take to academic work, and because of his great size was always out of place with the boys in his classes. He finished the 8th grade last year and is now attending a school where he is being taught mechanical knowledge in aviation. This is his first year, and he seems very well satisfied with his work. The other son, Max, is a nervous type, quick and alert. He is in the 7th grade and is very bright and alert in school.

Employment.—Mr. T learned the cleaning and dyeing business in Boston when he was apprenticed to his uncle who owned a cleaning and dyeing establishment. When Mr. T came to settle in Philadelphia after his marriage in 1918, he was employed by a cleaning and dyeing establishment as operator's helper for $35 per week. This employment lasted until 1920. From 1920 to 1924 Mr. T owned a cleaning and dyeing business. His earnings amounted to $25 per week. Mr. T sold this business in February, 1924, and opened a similar business. This business was again sold in 1927, and another establishment was opened. Mr. T remained here until 1929, when he sold out and opened another place of business. Here, Mr. T remained until August 1, 1934, at which time he again sold his business. Mr. T said that his business was coming along very nicely until 1934, when he felt that he could not continue any longer because of the Code. He had kept the spirit and letter of the Code while others cut their prices. Consequently he lost all the business he did have and failed to get new business. He sold the fixtures of this store on October 1, 1934, for $150, borrowed $150 more from his cousin, and opened another cleaning and pressing business at 1969 Melrose Avenue. This business lasted only a month and was closed on November 5, 1934.

Debts.—Mr. T has the following debts, some of which have been incurred before he closed his business. . . .

Relatives.—The older T is employed only part-time, and his earnings average $5 to $10 per week.

Norman, brother of Mr. T. He is working only part-time, is married and has three children.

Edgar, cousin of Mrs. T. He is married and has two children. His income was not known to Mr. T, who told the worker that he had helped him to the limit.

Maintenance and Resources.—During the past year Mr. T has maintained himself and family on the money borrowed from relatives. The only resources the family have are some insurance policies. They were taken out with the Life Insurance Company and are as follows . . .

These are the only resources reported by Mr. and Mrs. T to investigator, as they had never had a bank account.

Health.—Mrs. T was operated on four months ago at the General Hospital for tumor. Although she appears to be in very good health at the present time, she seems to be high-strung and nervous, which is probably a result of her operation. Mr. T has been ill for 8 years, suffering from an ulcer of the stomach. He has been treated for this condition at the Standard Hospital, Card No. 0059. He appears to be ill, and his face is worn with care and worry.

Problems.—The problems of the T family are not only unemployment but also poor health. When worker visited home there was no food in the house at all, and although there are potential assets, family appears destitute.

Worker recommends emergency relief; for budget see Financial and Social Data card.

HOME VISIT

Chronological Method

Pears, John, 2/6/35

Call was made in response to Mr. Pears' application for relief. Mrs. P, a small, tired-appearing woman, greeted visitor. She seemed tense and quite fortified for a "battle." Mr. P and his mother-in-law, Mrs. Walsh, were called. All seated themselves about the dining-room table and settled down to a pronounced silence, waiting for visitor to take the first step.

Visitor said she understood Mr. and Mrs. P had made application for relief, and she wondered if they would like to discuss their plans. Mrs. P was of the opinion that visitor had come to tell them "what to do," as they were going to move from this home to start housekeeping for themselves. Mr. P wanted to know how much rent he and his family would be allowed and when they could make the move. Visitor asked why Mr. and Mrs. P had decided to make a change. Mrs. P became very excited and stated that her mother could not care for them indefinitely and that they had to go. Mrs. Walsh did not enter into the conversation.

Visitor wondered what had caused the family to come to this decision at this time. Mrs. P then began to talk in a loud, excited voice again emphasizing the fact that her mother had cared for them for three years and could not do so any longer.

She pointed out that Mr. P was ill and had been for a long time. His diet was expensive, and his possibilities for work were small. Mr. P who had appeared quite "up to the situation," now confronted with his inadequacies, slumped in his chair and took on a helpless abused air, seeming willing to leave the whole matter to his wife.

Mrs. P continued that the income in the family was very small and that if she and her husband were to remain in the home, the whole family would have to ask for help. Visitor suggested that a budget for the P and Walsh families be worked out. Mrs. P objected. Her mother was not asking for help, and she saw no necessity for a combined budget. Visitor did not push the matter but spoke again of the P's expense upon Mrs. Walsh saying she understood how difficult this situation must be, but that many other families had been forced to make the same arrangement. For the first time Mrs. Walsh spoke. She felt the same way and would keep the P's if some help were given them. Visitor asked what the outstanding difficulty seemed to be. Mrs. Walsh believed that they could manage if it were not for Mr. P's diet which ran the grocery bills as high as $15 a week. Mr. and Mrs. Pears seemed utterly disgusted that the mother had made such a suggestion and objected to any plan of granting them aid in this home. Mr. P insisted that visitor tell them what to do. Visitor asked if Mr. P felt he could accept a plan visitor might make and suggested that he make his own decision. Mrs. P's excitement seemed to turn quickly into anger, and in her temper she gave the following information: Mr. Walsh died two years ago, leaving a small amount of insurance. After paying for burial expenses, there was only a small portion (approximately $200) left. This had been used to supplement the earnings of a daughter, Betty, who earns $15 a week at the Prudential Life Insurance Company, and Jerry, who at present averages $10 a week as a mover with some storage company. Now the insurance company money is gone, and the family does not see how they can manage on what Betty and Jerry earn. From the discussion of expenses in which both participated, visitor could see that the income did not cover their expenses. Mrs. Pears suggested that "we just figure it out to see." Mr. P asked if Home Relief budget was the same as the estimate. A Home Relief budget was then carefully explained.

Client's Estimate[6]		E. R. A. Budget	
Rent	$13.50	$ 8.30	
Food	30.00	15.90 (inc. special diet)	
Electricity	1.50	.65	
Gas (cooking) (heating)	4.00	2.40	
Carfare	1.20	1.20	
Clothing	4.00	4.00	
Lunches	3.00	3.60	
Insurance	5.00	. . .	
Incidentals	.50	.50	
	62.70	36.55	
Income	50.00	50.00	
Deficit	$12.70	Surplus	$13.45

Mrs. P became very excited over the surplus which the budget showed. Mrs. W did not believe it was possible to manage on such figures and remarked that her married daughter had to help with rent to keep the family out of debt. Mrs. P said this help from relatives could not continue. They now owe money borrowed when Mr. P had his operation in January. "After all," she added, "they are not legally responsible." Mr. P sighed, saying he did not understand how visitor could ask a family to lower its standards of living to such a degree that it was necessary to live like "gutter rats." He wants a job but does not believe he can work for several weeks yet. This seemed to be an attempt to draw himself into picture favorably. Mr. and Mrs. P and Mrs. W seemed confused, conflicting on various plans that suggested themselves. Visitor suggested that Mr. and Mrs. P think through the whole matter, discuss the situation with Mrs. Walsh, who offered them continued use of the home, and that visitor would return at a later date.

Eligibility procedures and successive contacts in de-

[6] Ordinarily the budget would be worked out on the appropriate card and only comment or total or both appear in the text. The reason for inclusion here is patent.

termining the need situation may be summarized whenever the material gained is largely of a business-like or
routine quality. One admitted reason that investigators
are asked to record a routine procedure step by step is
as a check on the untrained worker. It is important that
the sources of the information or contacts be made
clear by a "list of contacts" or parenthetically in connection with the facts reported if summary rather than
diary method is used. Comments and directions given
untrained workers by supervisors, as earlier noted, such
as: "Man apparently has resources, why is not bank
clearing made?" or "Arrange about medical examination for Georgia," do not belong in the permanent
record.

Follow-up contacts may or may not be summarized,
significant attitudes toward relief or re-employment
being always noted. Analyses of problems or other services undertaken in connection with relief administration differ in no way, except perhaps in brevity, from
other recording. In mothers' allowance cases, as in other
child welfare areas in which health supervision may be
practiced, outline or graphic forms to show progress or
growth have occasional value. Comments on significant
deviations should be noted in the text or in the periodic
summary, not on the form which gives the health or
school record. Workers who use periodic summaries
must keep their case notebooks current or the summaries will be sterile. Sometimes scratch long-hand
notes are filed in the record pending dictation. Such
notes should be clipped in, not filed loose, and they
should be destroyed after typing. In all times of acute
disturbance, especially if the agency is assuming responsibility for active treatment, chronological recording is

apt to be more reliable. The writer can, however, return to the summary for the mild and uneventful stretches of supervision, thus avoiding repetition and the futility of padding with trivial remarks.

Work histories are as specifically factual as possible, as are accounts of resources. One does not record "man had always had good jobs," but:

Mr. S worked for the Xavier Stone Co., Jones Street, by the river from 10/12/25 to 6/27, as engineer and draughtsman at $80 per week. Worked for Boston Marble Co., 13th St. & Dale Ave., from 1927 to 1929 as superintendent of the stoneyard at $90 per week. Then on January 10, 1929, he went back to the Xavier Stone Co. and worked there again as engineer and draughtsman up to January, 1932, at $67 per week. From June, 1932, to December, 1933, off and on, worked at odd jobs and also for Xavier Stone Co. at $50 per week, his last job being in December, 1933. References from the above companies described him as reliable and industrious and said that he would be rehired when work was available.

An example of routine follow-up is the following:

PERIODIC SUMMARY

3- 9-34 3-16-34 3-23-34 3-30-34 4-10-34 4-19-34	Grocery orders to the amount of $6.75 each delivered to client. Belleville also supplying 1 quart of milk daily throughout this period; government food orders also included. ½ ton of coal supplied March 13.

There is no change in the economic situation in this family. Arrangements, however, were made through Emergency Relief Bureau to provide dental treatment for John who was suffering with toothache and needed dental care. Mr. S is still endeavoring to make plans for the coal business, which if they succeed will provide employment for him beginning this coming fall. May has been transferred to the RCA factory but fortunately has not been laid off as yet. Clarence shows some slight improvement and has had one attack of *petit mal* but none of *grand mal* since his treatments at the Clinic. This is a decided improvement.

Diagnostic statements or interpretations of the relief problem may be of a simple situational type, of this order,

INTERPRETATION[7] (*Diagnostic Statement*)

This is the case of a young ex-miner and his wife with irregular job history since the shut-down of the mines six years ago. The couple is now living in a furnished room. All resources are exhausted, since the cousins with whom they have been living are now themselves on home relief. The man has an occupational handicap for heavy labor (chronic pulmonary tuberculosis arrested) , is markedly run down, anxious, and discouraged.

Since the couple are devoted to each other and the wife has a good record as domestic, it is possible that a living-in job can be arranged while the man's strength is being built up.

INTERPRETATION[7] (*Diagnostic Statement*)

The initial problem of unemployment in this artisan family is the chief causal factor of the related problems of health and morale.

Mr. B attributes his lack of employment for the past three years to the fact that the depression has most seriously affected men skilled in the building trades.

Mrs. B's physical disabilities of gastric disorder and rheumatism are exaggerated by her. She feels that her condition is not understood. She is highly dramatic, nervous, and irritable with her family. She laments the loss of the family's past comfortable income, her husband's present lack of work, the needs of the children, but she is particularly concerned with herself. She dominates the family group by emphasizing the seriousness of her condition and her need of attention.

She has trained her mild-mannered husband to become her obedient nurse and housekeeper. The children, naturally re-

---

[7] Compare diagnostic statements on page 56, but note that the phrase may not be acceptable in certain administrative agencies so that "interpretation" or some such word may be substituted as here.

spectful to their parents, scurry about the house to execute her orders. Although she wants Mr. B to work and "bring home the money as he used to" she does not consider it worth while for him to do unskilled labor at small wages. She would rather have him at home to take care of her. Mr. B's passive attitude indicates that he is not averse to this arrangement.

An example of clear recording of eligibility data, with analysis of investigation, that is, a sort of diagnostic statement and plan of treatment from an old-age-assistance case follows:

ELIGIBILITY SUMMARY

AGE		Born	Baptized	Verified
	Fannie................	10-2-63	10-6-63	Records of
	Margaret...............	1-24-61	1-31-61	St. Peter's
	Ruth.................	8-30-59	9-22-59	Church

BIRTH-PLACE:	Northside, Pittsburgh	BUDGETS:	Miss F.	Miss M.	Miss R.
	Verified by family record	Rent	$ 0	$ 0	$15
	and baptismal certificates	Food	9	9	9
		Fuel	2	2	2
RESIDENCE:	Life residence verified by	Clothing	4	4	4
	testimony of references				
			$15	$15	$30

RESOURCES: $250 cash held by Miss R.
    Affidavit in file.

Verification.—Housing conditions are crowded and not healthful. The only heat used is gas heat, and the house is, therefore, very damp. The household furnishings are old, and many of them are completely worn out. The Misses Bauer have saved all their possessions, and the rooms are overcrowded. Their health needs immediate attention. All three sisters have severe coughs, and Miss F frequently has fainting spells. Miss M is extremely nervous and seldom leaves the house. Their personal appearance marks them as "queer" and probably causes much comment among friends and neighbors. They have been extremely economical, to the point of starvation. They are all very thin and worn in appearance. There seems to be little acceptance of their present circumstances by any of the sisters. They were very anxious to impress V with their personal qualifications and the financial success of their parents. It was apparent that the Misses Bauer are extremely withdrawn and that they are unable to face their present situation. They react by disregarding their present circumstances and living in the past. The fact that they have applied for assistance seems disgraceful to them, and they were unable to accept it sufficiently to cooperate during the investigation.

PLAN

Attempt to gain the confidence of the Misses Bauer in order that they may feel free to discuss their problems.

By interpretation, help them to accept OAA so that the feelings of disgrace and shame connected with it may be eliminated.

Arrange for medical treatment by first preparing them to realize the need for care. Arrange for necessary follow-up attention.

Assist in budgeting finances, with special emphasis on food habits. Encourage the family to eat sufficiently and to use nourishing foods.

Attempt to establish some recreational interests.

Below is shown interviewing in a relief situation described in modified "process" style. The familiar circumstances probably justify such careful recording, but ordinarily so much reproduction would be inappropriate and condensation would be preferable.

CHRONOLOGICAL RECORDING

Modified process

10-13-33: Mrs. P came to get the remainder of the money. She felt that it was hard to manage, but she thinks it is going better. She is glad to have the whole amount, as she is able to save by buying larger amounts of staples. Worker said that she knew it was hard to manage, and now that ice money must be deducted it would take away a little more. Worker would be glad to talk over any questions of how saving could be made if she wanted to keep a list of expenditures. According to the new budget the food allowance came to $6.73. This was explained to her. 80¢ a week was added for cleaning and household supplies. She seemed appalled by stretching $7.53 to cover this. Again she mentioned how much money milk and meat take. She had tried using more evaporated milk.

She brought out four insurance policies which she wanted to discuss. She said, "I did not tell you before, but my aunt in Porto Rico sent me $5 last week." With this she had bought a felt hat for 35¢, stockings for herself and the children and had made some insurance payments. These had been carried in the past by her aunt, who now cannot assume this regularly. She said, "You do not pay insurance," in a questioning voice. Worker said that this was true, but sometimes we could help by securing an adjustment. This is what she had in mind. She had talked with the agent, who said that nothing could be done and pressed her for back payments, threatening her with a loss of the policies. Worker said that she could not help her with this unless she also brought in her books showing the date of payments, etc. She agreed to do this. Neither her husband nor George has insurance. Mr. P does not believe in it. She said tentatively, "Maybe it is not a good thing for people in our circumstances to carry it." Worker asked why she thought so. When her husband had a job or her aunt could pay, it was different. Perhaps insurance is only for people with jobs. She hated to let it go, though. "It seems like savings. He would never save any other way." Her idea was to have 15 or 20 year endowment for her children starting at 1 year. "I hope they will be intelligent and want an education. The money would help just when they need it." She did not mention the value of having funeral expenses guaranteed. Worker asked if she might copy the data from the policies. . . . (Full data omitted.)

10-24-33: Mr. P in office three-quarters of an hour late. He announced dramatically, "I have some good news. I have a job." Worker expressed interest. He added, "But not in New York," watching worker closely. He drew out a letter from his pocket from a friend, Mr. Baba, in Honduras, Central America, offering him a permanent job at $100 a month plus maintenance, to manage a restaurant. Mr. Baba is down there now. He wishes to install a soda fountain and luncheonette and wants Mr. P because of his experience. He also had another commission to discuss with a manufacturer of ice machines. There is some question of the transportation of this machinery to Honduras immediately. Worker asked how he planned to get there. Mr. P looked at worker questioningly. He said, "That's just it. I wondered if you would help me." Worker said that we were unable to help people in this way. He said that he had thought so. However, he was asking Mr. Baba to pay his transportation fare of $60 to $80 out of his salary. He thought this could be arranged.

Worker asked what Mrs. P thought of this opportunity. He hastily explained that he did not intend to take his family. The climate would be too hard. The schools were not good. "You know, I think only of my children. I think of their future. I would not sacrifice them." Worker made no answer. Mr. P moved uneasily in his chair. He was looking very anxious and guilty. He went on that of course he would send back sufficient to support his family. He never forgets that he has responsibilities. Worker said nothing for a minute and finally asked, "You really want to leave your family, don't you?" He replied affirmatively in a low voice. Worker said that as it was very late today, it did not seem possible to discuss all that this might mean. Perhaps he would want to come in on Saturday after thinking it over and discuss it further. He agreed. . . .

Later: Mrs. P was seen. . . . Worker asked what she thought of Mr. P's plan. She said that she would never stop him. Worker asked if she wanted him to leave her. She shrugged her shoulders. She feels that his leaving is inevitable, whether in New York or elsewhere. About four months ago Mr. Baba joined his brother in Honduras, who owns a large gambling casino. She thinks that this luncheon counter of which Mr. P speaks is in connection with the gambling establishment. "I tell you that he likes to gamble," she said. She believes that Mr. Baba is reliable and would pay the salary as he agreed.

Worker wondered if Mr. P might find it hard to send her money for support for herself and the children. Mrs. P thought it unlikely that he would do this for long. "But what can I do? I can't ask you. He should be ashamed that we have to come for charity for two years. If he goes, I will go to work. I used to work." Worker asked how she planned to manage about the children. She would place the two older boys and keep the two younger ones, placing them in a nursery in the daytime. She spoke of all this with a kind of excited interest that implied her willingness to separate. Worker asked if she thought things would be happier if they separated. She agreed heartily to this.

She was much worried about how they could get on if Mr. P failed to send her money. Worker said that if Mr. Baba paid Mr. P's passage he might not be able to send her much the first month. She said by that time she wouldn't have to go to clinics as she would be well. Worker said that this was something we could talk over at the hospital.

Mrs. P said, "My father is mad at him." She repeated material previously given regarding their home in Porto Rico, her mother's death when she was 11, and her father's remarriage, which made family life very unhappy for her until she was 15 and left home to go to work. She described her father's independence. He would never get into a situation where he had to ask for charity. Worker said, "That was the kind of a man you wanted to marry, wasn't it?" She said, "Oh yes," with a discouraged sigh, "but I didn't get it. I guess I will get on all right alone."

She spoke of a desire to get a cash return from her insurance policy. She needs money for blankets, towels, sheets, pillow slips, diapers, as well as clothing for winter. All the household things have been worn out. "After two years and no work, what could you expect?" In the interview today, she did not seem as confused as sometimes noted. She was alert throughout. Surprisingly little feeling was exhibited at any point.

Services and treatment in public-assistance records are recorded as in any other agency, with the usual warning about simplicity and condensation.

There is not much to be said further about style in public-assistance records other than the caution, in general, to avoid "process" and any diction which is ostentatious or imitative of the latest fashion in case-work terminology. Steering blanks for reports from one agency to another, like forms, have their place and, although rigid, are justifiably time-saving in uncomplicated situations. The content of the blank follows the formula of the ordinary letter of inquiry, namely, identifying data; the nature of Agency A's contact—in this field the type and plan of assistance always being described; problems emerging of interest to Agency B, with a request for clarification of, or coöperation on, the shared problems; and a section left for the return report. See Chapter V. In complicated situations a letter which individualizes the case is preferable. People sometimes ask what they should record about their own contact with the family. It seems clear that Agency A has no right to ask a report of Agency B, assuming that both are professional agencies, unless Agency A is willing to give its reason for the inquiry. This reason should be contained in a succinct explanation of what Agency A is doing for the family. It is unnecessary for either agency to tell all it knows, but each should offer its coöperating colleague whatever bears on the *shared or intersecting areas* of the problem under discussion. Public-assistance agencies should not, especially since their records are subject to relatively wide staff reading, object to receiving reports which appear to be based upon the economic-social situation and relevant factors. Nor, indeed, should any agency resent carefully selected and restrained reports. If more information is required, as it is in occasional cases, and if the reason for asking it is proper, any agency would be obligated by professional courtesy to supply a further report either by letter or in conference; but it would not be obligated to allow its records to be read unless it wishes to do so.

The writer does not believe in a graded scale of secrecy in which Agency A tells all it knows, Agency B a little less than it knows, and Agency C nothing if it can be avoided. Some clients like to discuss their emotional problems and are sensitive about their financial ones; of others the reverse is true, so that we must consider their feelings about the subject. The client has a right in all cases to the maximum of protection; but since the social work area is typically complex, more than one agency may be legitimately involved, and essential information must be shared by appropriate agencies. Professional ethics demand: a discriminating relevance of detail, which is, in effect, reticence; and the consent of the client, whenever practicable, before inquiries are made on his behalf. There are matters which are properly regarded by the client and accepted by the worker as absolutely confidential, and these should not be disclosed without the client's consent. The public-assistance field, more than most fields, has suffered from two extremes. The former, deriving from old deterrent and stigmatic attitudes, would expose the relief recipient to every prying curiosity; the latter, isolated from professional practice, would be unwilling even to use the social-service exchange. This is not an argument for one hundred percent clearing in the social work community because the writer believes, for certain fields, in selective registration. In public, family, children's, and protective work, however, regular clearing and registration are important, except that if the name of the department which is registering defines a particular problem, such as illegitimacy, extra precautions should be taken in the use of any central index.

To summarize, the public agency will lean more on forms than will the private, and in the use of forms workers must be trained to a real interest in and accuracy about details of budget and relief granted. Forms should be combined so far as possible to avoid duplication of data, should be standardized as to shape, and should have uniform arrangements for similar material. In relief administration the illusion that most cases are alike can be dispelled by practice in interpretation or diagnostic statement. Although forms and steering blanks may be appropriate for employment, health, and school inquiries, the corresponding danger of a futile rubber-stamp request for "a report of your contact" should be recognized. It is important for the public agency not only to interpret the case within the record but also to be able to interpret its service to individuals and agencies in the community. Good letters and reports and intelligent inquiries are as necessary in relief administration as in other fields.

The arrangement of the record should be most often chronological, with summaries whenever the subject matter warrants—eligibility and periodic summaries being among the more usable types. Modified "process" may be sparingly used and only for unusually significant interviews. For most purposes a sharply condensed narrative style is desirable.

There is no great difference between the recording in relief administration and that in other case-work agencies except that the financial aspects will be stressed and that a larger proportion of records will be short, direct, and uncomplicated, because many public-assistance cases are uncomplicated. The chief factor which most distinguishes the public- from the private-agency record will be the amount of "administrative" material, arising out of the legal framework and the necessary body of regulations. This material must be included, but it should not obscure the development of social study and service. This pervasive "administrative" element must not be confused with procedures which should be reduced to a minimum. Not only bookkeeping, but also appointments, bills, and mechanics still

clutter the average public record. In domestic relations
court we may see the same overloading of the record
with routine reports of collections of payments, and
medical-social records are all-too-frequently limited to
financial and institutional routine. In the less-well-
established social agencies, records may be used almost
wholly for these mechanical items rather than for other
case-work purposes; but as the professional content
deepens, certain details will be separated from the others and handled through supplementary record devices.
The subordination of the business and executive elements to social case work can be achieved in the record
only if case load, training, and program allow for case
work in practice. When we say case work, we do not
mean something subtle and attenuated. To treat human
beings as individuals, not by rote or by pattern, to indi-
vidualize them by budget, by interview, by consideration of the relevant factors in their economic and
personal situation, this makes relief administration one
of the recognized fields of case work and lifts recording
out of the perfunctory and into the significant.

X

CONCLUSION

"READING maketh a full man, conference a ready man and writing an exact man," said Bacon. Unfortunately as knowledge of a subject grows it is hard for the writer of a journal or record to retain simplicity as well as truth. If language could represent all our knowledge, a record would indeed be of real use. The case worker is nothing if he has not a broad human view based on close, and one may say, loving interest in the drama of existence. The case worker who is not curious about people and concerned about helping them will never be a great case worker, but his professional discipline is yet "to abstain, to distinguish, to prefer," recognizing the limitations, not of the life experience itself which can have no exact boundaries, but those of his own rôle. This is just as true of recording. To workers who say anxiously, should we not put in everything in the event that some of it later may prove important, the answer is that we should study again and again not merely complicated situations but the obvious and the dull to be sure that significance has not eluded us, and that which we see is our business. After such sifting, what we then choose as probably relevant belongs in the case record. Effective recording like effective listening is always an active process of attention and selection. "It is not the recording," as a wise case worker once said, "which is difficult; it is the thinking which precedes it." If we can think clearly about the client's needs, his circumstances, and the treatment proposed, the record will shape itself easily and simply.

Today case recording in all fields represents certain generic features. All records deal with the processes of diagnosis and treatment, arbitrarily arranged. Records in all fields use similar face cards, forms, and outlines, and the physical format is roughly comparable. Differential features are resultant from administrative considerations, major functional emphases and the relative emphasis given to the requirements of practice, teaching, and research, with practice the dominant consideration in most agencies. Records differ more from agency to agency than from field to field, and differ markedly within agencies from worker to worker. The treatment focus tends to make for selection of material around the problem presented and the reaction of the client to his problem. The development in the social science laboratory in the testing of attitudes, behavior or other measurements, does not yet permit of much adaptation for case records, so that the case record remains today an informal journal rather than an instrument of precision.

For the material found in case records both diary and summary method are in good usage—the conscious selection of either method depending on its appropriateness. Most records show combining forms of the diary, or chronological, entry with occasional summaries either in abstracts or in topical arrangements. Although records have been recently greatly expanded through the recording of interviewing process, this may be regarded as an expense chargeable to experimental purposes, and already there is evidence of selection in place of verbatim reproduction of the whole interview.

The client's own story in his own words has lately been given prominence in the record, and close attention to behavior has resulted in a more vigorous and readable narrative. Incidents which show social relations and personal feelings as well as the familiar facts of physical setting now find a place. The rôle of the worker in service or treatment is indicated; process in treatment is sometimes fully described. The best case work, however, is the most natural, and the best recording does not labor the obvious.

Letters and reports, under the influence of a better diagnostic approach and better treatment controls, show a clearer problem sense. Letters now tend to try to answer what the correspondent wants to know, which is usually what the immediate situation is and what has been or is being done about it, and not to give a summary of the entire case unless this is really appropriate and necessary. Both in social study and in letters history has been subordinated to the needs which the client presents, and the growth of coöperative case handling keeps the tone of letters from insisting on the last word as the older letters seemed often to do.

Diagnostic thinking in all forms is still inadequate, but progress is marked. Purely factual recapitulation is yielding to interpretation and evaluation as skill among case workers is increasing. Inferences, impressions, problem configurations, diagnostic statement, and diagnostic discussion and evaluation are indispensable in the treatment record, and it is only the "roughness of the eye" which makes us unable to see significances in everyday experiences. This does not mean that we should read into situations things that are not there or, if there, do not concern us, but that we should try to express as clearly as possible the meaning of each case for us as practitioners. Style remains individual, with values always in brevity and lucidity. Records are now more objective in reporting data, more precise in concept and terminology than formerly.

It is now understood that the records should be built up in advance for special research inquiries and that the ex post facto use of records for widely varied demands will not be productive. Records used in the supervision of students are apt to be longer than necessary for practice alone, and the cost here must be assigned partly to training purposes. Records used in classroom teaching are frequently edited to reduce the bulk; also the practice of using excerpts, interviews instead of whole records, is growing. The problem of naming, defining, and quantifying social data is still unsolved.

At present records are costly to write and to read. As advances are made in social case work, it is hoped that the professional record will become increasingly selective. A good record would be that in which, issues having been apprehended early, there is a minimum of fact or thinking irrelevant to the problems under consideration. In the hands of the skilled practitioner, only such material, after the initial study, would be recorded as has bearing on shifts in the hypothesis, with more accurate interpretation and with corresponding developments or changes in treatment. In an ultimate sense only the trained diagnostician can write a good record, for only he can pluck from the unending web of social experience the thread of probable significance.

GLOSSARY OF RECORDING TERMS

CHRONOLOGICAL RECORDING: Entries arranged according to the order of the calendar; comparable to diary method. Within the dated entry the material may be recorded as it happened in time sequence or it may be topically arranged. In general, chronological recording is opposed to summarized recording, and topical methods are opposed to narrative and process styles.

CLOSING ENTRY: A short summary containing selected situation data, significant problems and treatment, but with the emphasis on course and results of treatment.

DIAGNOSTIC STATEMENT: A brief definition of the interrelated difficulties. This configuration describes only proximate or immediate interacting causal factors. The present tense is preferred. Prognosis and estimate of treatability may be included.

DIAGNOSTIC SUMMARY: Contains historical and situation data. The interpretation is suggested in part by the selection of findings and in part by diagnostic comment. A paragraph on treatment proposed or in retrospect is often included and also prognosis. Earlier diagnostic summaries were little more than social histories. Current diagnostic summaries are often elaborate affairs, proposed for or reflecting staff discussions. Such elaborate summaries are more usually called "diagnostic discussions" or staff conferences.

DIAGNOSTIC THINKING: Informal interpretations or impressions associated with the text of the interview, characteristic in process style of recording.

FINDINGS: Significant data obtained from the study of the situation and the history, listed or grouped, but not interrelated. Findings may be positive or negative; they constitute the raw material of diagnosis and prognosis.

INTERVAL HISTORY: Covers the period between applications.

PERIODIC SUMMARY: Account of case while under care, made at regular or irregular intervals. May be either a digest of previously recorded material or a digest from case-study notes. If appraisal of treatment rather than account of treatment is the characteristic, "treatment evaluation" is preferred. May be in topical or narrative or part-process style.

PROCESS METHOD: An extension of the chronological method; the recording of each entry in time sequence, giving a verbatim reproduction of the interview. May include diagnostic impressions associated with the interview. In long interviews, parts may be selected for the "process" style, and in periodic summaries parts of several interviews may be reproduced in the same way.

SOCIAL HISTORY: A summary from the life experience preceding the application, although the current situation is customarily included. Usually topical. May be derived from historical material already in the record or from case-study notes.

SUMMARY: An abridged account; an abstract; a digest of material which has previously appeared in the case record; less commonly, a digest from case notes which have not previously appeared in the case record.

TOPICAL RECORDING: The organization of material under headings, either within a single interview or for a period. Summaries are usually, but not always, topical. Condensation of interviews derived from a process method are selected to follow time sequence and are not usually topical.

TRANSFER SUMMARY: Same as "closing entry," but usually fuller because case is still active.

TREATMENT EVALUATION: A periodic or occasional summary describing and analyzing course of treatment, methods used, reactions to treatment, progress, and so forth, and usually planning for further treatment and prognosis. It may or may not include detailed comment on technique.

BIBLIOGRAPHY

American Association of Social Workers, Milford Conference, Social Case Work, Generic and Specific. American Association of Social Workers, New York, 1929.

American Public Welfare Association, Recording and Reporting with Regard to Old Age Assistance. Chicago, 1935.

Breckinridge, S. P., Medical Social Case Records. University of Chicago Press, Chicago, 1928.

Bristol, Margaret C., Handbook on Social Case Recording, The University of Chicago Press, Chicago, 1936.

Bruno, Frank J., Some Case Work Recording Limitations of Verbatim Reporting. *Journal of Social Forces,* Vol. VI, No. 4, June, 1928.

Cabot, Richard C., Social Work, Houghton Mifflin, Boston, 1919.

Cannon, M. A., and Klein, P., Social Case Work, Columbia University Press, New York, 1933.

Charity Organization Society, Social Case Histories. Printed by the Charity Organization Department of Russell Sage Foundation, New York, Vol. III, December, 1911.

Chase, Stuart A., Can Interviews Be Described Objectively? *Journal of Social Forces,* Vol. VII, No. 4, June, 1929.

Clark, Mary A., Recording and Reporting for Child Guidance Clinics. Commonwealth Fund, Division of Publications, New York, 1930.

Corscaden, James Albert, History Taking and Recording. Hoeber, New York, 1926.

Culbert, Jane F., The Visiting Teacher. Commonwealth Fund, Division of Publications, Reprint Series No. 1, New York, 1929.

Dawley, Almena, Diagnosis—the Dynamic of Effective Treatment, *The Journal of Social Work Process,* Vol. I, No. 1, The Pennsylvania School of Social Work, Philadelphia, 1937.

Eliot, Thomas D., Objectivity and Subjectivity in the Case

Record. *Journal of Social Forces,* Vol. VI, No. 4, June, 1928.

Family Welfare Association of America, Report of Recording Committee, Milwaukee, September, 1934.

Farmer, Gertrude L., Form of Record for Hospital Social Work, Including Suggestions for Organization. Lippincott, Philadelphia, 1921.

Fisk, H. I., Statistical Recording and Reporting in Family Welfare Agencies. Family Welfare Association of America, New York, 1934.

Fowler, H. W. and F. T., The King's English. Oxford, Clarendon Press, New York, 1922.

Gartland, Ruth M., Psychiatric Social Service in a Children's Hospital, The University of Chicago Social Service Monographs, The University of Chicago Press, Chicago, 1937.

Hall, Beatrice, The Social Service Record in the Unit Medical History. *Hospital Social Service Magazine,* Vol. XX, No. 1, July, 1929.

Hamilton, Gordon, A Medical Social Terminology. Presbyterian Hospital, New York City, 1930.

—— Notes on Current Practices in Medical Social Case Recording. *The Family,* Vol. XII, No. 3, May, 1931.

Isaacs, Susan, Social Development in Young Children. Harcourt, Brace and Co., New York, 1933.

Judge Baker Foundation, Case Studies. The Foundation, Series No. 1, Boston, 1922.

Karpf, Maurice J., Sociologists and Social Workers Meet. *The Family,* Vol. IX, No. 2, April, 1928.

Lee, P. R., and Kenworthy, M. E., Mental Hygiene and Social Work. Commonwealth Fund, Division of Publications, New York, 1929.

Lundberg, George A., Case Work and the Statistical Method. *Journal of Social Forces,* Vol. V, No. 1, September, 1926.

—— Social Research, a Study in Methods of Gathering Data. Longmans, Green & Co., New York, 1929.

Phelps, Harold A., The Case Record and Scientific Method. *The Family,* Vol. VIII, No. 4, June, 1927.

Queen, Stuart A., Elements of Record Keeping for Child-Helping Organizations. N. Y. Survey Associates, New York, 1915.

Reynolds, Bertha E., Between Client and Community. Smith

College Studies in Social Work, Vol. V, No. 1, September, 1934.

Richmond, Mary, Social Diagnosis. Russell Sage Foundation, New York, 1917.

Robinson, Virginia P., Analysis of Processes in the Records of Family Case Working Agencies. *The Family,* Vol. II, No. 5, July, 1921.

—— A Changing Psychology in Social Case Work. University of North Carolina Press, Chapel Hill, N. C., 1934.

Ruhland, G. C. and Thompson, I. F., Record Forms in the Syracuse Health Demonstration. *American Journal of Public Health,* Vol. XVI, June, 1926.

Sheffield, Mrs. Ada E., Social Case History, Its Construction and Content. Russell Sage Foundation, New York, 1920.

—— The Situation As the Unit of Social Case Study. *Social Forces,* Vol. IX, No. 4, June, 1931.

Southard, E. E. and Jarrett, M., The Kingdom of Evils. Macmillan Company, New York, 1922.

Swift, Linton B., Can the Sociologist and the Social Worker Agree on the Content of Case Records? *Journal of Social Forces,* Vol. VI, No. 4, June, 1928.

Taft, Jessie, The Dynamics of Therapy in a Controlled Relationship. Macmillan, New York, 1933.

Tennant, Gertrude, Prize Medical Social Case Record. *Social Service Review,* Vol. I, No. 3, September, 1927.

U. S. Children's Bureau, Publication No. 101, Office Administration for Organizations Supervising the Health of Mothers, Infants and Children of Pre-School Age, by Estelle B. Hunter: *Planning Case Record Systems,* pp. 52-70; *Statistics,* pp. 70-76; and *Record Filing,* pp. 77-91. 1922.

—— Publication No. 171, The Work of Child-Placing Agencies: *Recording the Successes and Failures of Foster Homes,* pp. 49-50, 1927.

Wajdyk, Beatrice H., An Intensive Treatment Approach, Differential Approach in Case Work Treatment, Family Welfare Association of America, 1936.

Waller, Willard, Insight and Scientific Method. *American Journal of Sociology,* Vol. XI, No. 3, November, 1934.

Weed, Margaret, Recent Changes in Record Writing. *The Family,* Vol. XIII, No. 3, May, 1932.

Young, Erle F., Scientific Study of Social Case Records, *Journal of Applied Sociology,* Vol. IX, No. 4, March-April, 1925.
—— Provisional Manual of Directions for the American Council. Revised from *Educational Record Supplement,* No. 8, July, 1928.

INDEX